BEGINNER'S

TO

COOKING WITH SPICES

JOSEPH VEEBE

Books in this Series:

TABLE OF CONTENTS

Table of Contents 3

Chapter 1. Introduction 8

   Introduction..8

   History of Spices 9

   Turmeric...10

   Cinnamon..12

   Ginger..14

   Garlic 15

   Clove..16

   Cumin 17

   Fennel..18

   Chili Pepper and Chili Powder 18

   Cardamom...19

   Black Pepper..19

   Coriander..21

   Herbs..24

Chapter 2. Health Benefits of Spices and Herbs 28

   Anti-cancer Properties...28

   Anti-oxidant Properties..30

   Anti-inflammatory Benefits...31

   Immune System and Infections....................................32

   Arthritis..33

   Neuro-Protective...33

   Cholesterol..35

Pain 36

Improved Circulation 37

Anti-depressant 37

Gastrointestinal Benefits 37

Skin and Hair 37

Indigestion 38

Nausea and Morning Sickness 39

Diabetes and Heart Health 39

Lower Blood Pressure 40

Improved Physical Performance 40

Cold and Flu 41

Bone Health 41

Antibacterial and Anti-parasitic 41

Detox Agent 42

Chapter 3. Spice Mixes 43

Origin 43

Curry Powder 43

More South Asian Spice Mixes 45

Chinese, Japanese and Thai Spice mixes 47

African and Middle Eastern Spice Mixes 49

Americas and European Spice Mixes 51

Other Spice Mixes 52

Chapter 4. Tips for Cooking with Spices 54

Chapter 5. Cooking Vegan with Spices 60

Leafy Greens 60

Spinach / Red Chard......................................61

Spinach and potato.......................................62

Lentils & Beans...63

Spicy Chickpeas...64

Spicy Lentils and Kale....................................65

Vegetables...67

Cauliflower and Potato....................................67

Spicy Mashed Potato.......................................68

Spicy Steamed Broccoli....................................69

Eggplant Curry..70

Chapter 6. Fish and Meat Dishes...........................72

Fish..72

10 Minute Salmon Curry....................................72

Salmon with green mango...................................74

Fish Fry..76

Beef..77

Spicy Beef and Potato Stu.................................78

Beef and Cassava..79

Beef Pepper Fry...82

Chicken...83

Bell Pepper and Chicken Stir Fry..........................83

Coconut Curry Chicken.....................................84

Kale and Chicken Fry......................................86

Chapter 7. Spiced Rice Dishes.............................88

Tomato Rice...88

Yellow Rice with Peas...89

Chapter 8. Spicy Broths and Soups 92

Spicy Vegan Broth 92

Spicy Chicken Bone Broth 94

Bone Beef Broth 96

Lamb Bone Broth (Lamb Bones roasted)................98

Black Bean soup...99

Lentil Soup 100

Spicy Cream of Broccoli and Kale Soup...............101

Chapter 9. Additional Information 103

What not to Do with Spices 103

Where to Buy..106

References...108

Disclaimer 114

Preview of Other Books in this Series..........................116

Essential Spices and Herbs: Turmeric...................116

Preventing Cancer...117

Preventing Alzheimer's 118

All Natural Wellness Drinks.................................120

Introduction to Curry...120

Essential Spices and Herbs: Ginger 121

Essential Spices and Herbs: Garlic.......................122

Essential Spices and Herbs: Cinnamon.................122

Anti-Cancer Curries 123

Beginners Guide to Cooking with Spices..............123

Easy Indian Instant Pot Cookbook.....................................124

Fighting the Virus: How to Boost Your Body's Immune Response and Fight Virus Naturally....................................125

Easy Spicy Eggs: All Natural Easy and Spicy Egg Recipes..126

Food for the Brain..126

CHAPTER 1. INTRODUCTION

INTRODUCTION

I want to thank you for purchasing this book, "Beginner's Guide to Cooking with Spices." I have written books on several essential spices, as well as their medicinal and health benefits. Many of these books include recipes. I realized that a lot of people are still new to spices and a book on how to use them will be beneficial to many. This book contains a lot of information that you will find handy in your daily cooking adventures with spices.

Some of the spices used in modern times have been known to ancient civilizations and their health benefits are proven over thousands of years of use. Modern medicine has been increasingly studying many of these herbs and spices. However, many more organized studies are needed to get approval from the regulatory agencies for these herbs and spices to be accepted as part of mainstream prevention or treatment options for a number of medical conditions.

One thing is for sure - no one likes food that tastes bland. We all want to eat healthy and tasty food. But we are too busy to make fresh food at home. So, we settle for fast foods or packaged foods instead of healthy, homemade meals. The recipes listed in this book are quick and easy. The average time to cook is about 20 minutes.

This book is part of the "Essential Spices and Herbs" series. The book details use and benefits of many common and essential spices including turmeric, cinnamon, chili, cumin, coriander, and ginger, among others. Many of these spices have proven health benefits including fighting cancer, Alzheimer's, diabetes, pain, and much more.

The recipes are put together so that they can be easily prepared using common ingredients. There are several optional ingredients that you can try out to make the dish according to your personal taste and creativity.

HISTORY OF SPICES

Humans have used spices from the beginning of time. One can find references to various spices in ancient scripts such as the Old Testament, Bhagavad-Gita, and other writings. Ancient Egyptians, Chinese, Indians, Arabs, Greeks, and Romans have all used spices for various purposes, from cooking to food preservation and as medicine. There were many things that attracted humans to the use of spices – their aroma, their distinct taste and ability to flavor food, their color, and finally, their medicinal properties. Archaeologists discovered the use of spices as preservatives or offerings in ancient Egyptian tombs and in other excavations. There are records of many civilizations around the world using herbs and spices for common ailments such as wound healing, fever, microbial infections, and more.

Some fascinating history of these common spices is described below. Many of the other spices have a similar history and are too long to write about in this book.

Similar to turmeric and garlic, ginger use also dates back from 4000 to 5000 years by Indians and Chinese. Indians used ginger as a standalone flavoring ingredient in drinks such as buttermilk and ginger teas. Ginger was used in Ayurvedic medicine as a substance that helped with stomach ailments and nausea. Ginger was often used in conjunction with garlic and turmeric (in paste form) to flavor curries in Indian cuisine. Cardamom, cloves, and cinnamon similarly were used by ancient civilizations as well.

In summary, many of the spices described in this book have been used for over 4000 years by ancient Indians, Chinese, and Egyptians; either in conjunction or individually and have a rich history. There is some evidence that the Indus Valley civilization which was at its peak about 2500 BC used all kinds of spices – turmeric, cinnamon, coriander, garlic and ginger, and others. Some of these spices such as turmeric and cinnamon are also used as an important part of Ayurvedic medicine for diabetes treatment, wound healing, and treating infections. Below is a list of most beneficial spices:

TURMERIC

Turmeric is a well-known spice in Asian cooking, especially South Asia. Turmeric comes from the root of the turmeric plant which is part of the ginger family. The turmeric root is cleaned, dried, and grinded to create the yellow turmeric powder. Turmeric is used as an herbal supplement, added to flavor food as part of curry powder or as a standalone spice, added to cosmetics, or used as a food coloring. Turmeric is also used as a skin treatment and beauty enhancer. Evidently, it has been used by humans for thousands of years and is a time-tested wonder. This chapter will focus on turmeric and its benefits as part of food and cooking.

Turmeric powder is bright yellow and provides the distinct yellow color to the Indian "curry powder." Turmeric has been one of the key ingredients in Asian cuisine for years.

The main active ingredient in turmeric is called curcumin, which has very powerful medicinal properties. However, there are two challenges in fully realizing the benefits of turmeric. One, the curcumin content is only about 3% of turmeric by weight. Second, curcumin is not easily absorbed by the body. Curcumin absorption can be substantially enhanced by consuming black pepper which contains piperine along with turmeric. Also, fatty foods have been proven to aid curcumin absorption as well. To consume a sufficient dosage of curcumin, a combination of curcumin/turmeric extract supplements along with a diet prepared with turmeric is recommended.

Turmeric is a rich source of many essential vitamins and minerals; it does not contain any cholesterol but is an excellent source of antioxidants and dietary fiber which helps to control bad cholesterol levels.

Fresh turmeric root is a very good source of several vitamins such as vitamin-C, vitamin B-6, vitamin-E, and niacin. Turmeric is also a great source of several minerals such as calcium, iron, potassium, manganese, copper, zinc, and magnesium.

Turmeric's antioxidant levels are one of the highest among popular spices and herbs.

CINNAMON

Cinnamon (Cinnamomum *zeylanicum)* is one of the world's healthiest and oldest spices. Both ancient Chinese and ancient Egyptians used cinnamon as far back as 2500 B. C. Egyptians used it for embalming process of mummies due to its perfume as well as its preservative properties. Bible has reference to cinnamon as a perfuming agent in the preparation of anointing oils.

There are two kinds of cinnamon available on the market today; *verum* or "true" cinnamon is native to Sri Lanka (formerly Ceylon) and cassia cinnamon which is produced almost everywhere else (China, Malaysia, Vietnam, Bangladesh, India).

Historical evidence indicates that cinnamon was popular and in use by the ancient civilizations in the middle east and Asia. Arab traders introduced cinnamon to Europe during the middle ages but kept their source secret.

European's fell in love with cinnamon and demand started to significantly outweigh the supply from Arab traders. European explorers thus set out to find the source for cinnamon and also some of the other spices such as black pepper, cardamom, and others.

Portuguese traders were the ones to succeed first. In the early 16th century, Portuguese traders discovered cinnamon was abundant in present day Sri Lanka (formerly Ceylon).

Portuguese conquered Sri Lanka soon and controlled all the cinnamon supply and trade for the next century.

While Portuguese was enjoying the benefits of cinnamon trade, other European countries were not sitting idle. They had their own search to find the source of cinnamon and in the early to mid-17th century, the Dutch aligned with local Sri Lankan king and defeated Portuguese. Now the Dutch controlled cinnamon. They will continue that for the next 150 years until the 4th Anglo-Dutch war in 1784 when England took over Sri Lanka. Soon, Europeans and others realized that cinnamon could be cultivated in any tropical climate and started cultivating cinnamon tropical parts of the world controlled by them. Cinnamon ceased to be expensive and become more widely available. However, Sri Lanka or Ceylon cinnamon continues to be the original "true" cinnamon which is distinguished by milder and sweeter flavor. All other cinnamon is called cassia which is less expensive and of lower quality.

Cinnamon is used primarily in baking and is one of the healthiest spices. Cinnamon is packed with antioxidants, anti-inflammatory, anti-bacterial and anti-fungal agents. Cinnamon is good in fighting common infections due to its anti-microbial properties. Other benefits include lower and stabilize blood sugar levels in diabetes patients, lower cholesterol, and improve brain function. For more on cinnamon, please see my book titled "Essential Spices and Herbs: Cinnamon".

GINGER

Ginger (*Zingiber officinale*) is a flowering plant whose root is widely used as a spice and traditional medicine over thousands of years in Asia. Ginger belongs to the same family as turmeric and cardamom.

Ginger is widely used in Asian cooking, especially China and India. While turmeric, which belongs to the same family as ginger is mostly used in the powder form, ginger is used as a fresh ingredient in most cooking.

Ginger has been one of the key ingredients in Asian cuisine for centuries, especially used as part of meat recipes. When dried and ground, ginger results in a white powder that is used in baking (gingerbread, cookies, crackers, cakes etc.) and making beverages (ginger ale, ginger beer, etc.). Ginger, either powdered or fresh, can be used in teas and is an essential component of 'masala chai'.

The main bioactive active ingredient in ginger is called gingerol and it has very powerful medicinal properties. Ginger is used in several alternative/traditional medicines in the East.

Unlike turmeric, ginger is not a significant source of vitamins and minerals. More than 75% of raw ginger is water. Ginger does contain small amounts of minerals and vitamins as in the table below. The most important component of ginger is gingerol which provides its anti-oxidant and anti-inflammatory properties.

GARLIC

Garlic is believed to have originated in Central/West Asia. Ancient Indians have used it about 6000 years ago for its medicinal and aphrodisiac properties. Over the next thousand years, it spread to middle-east and Egypt to the Babylonian and Assyrian empires. Garlic was used in ancient times as a food seasoning and as a remedy for many common ailments. Romans and Egyptians fed garlic to warriors and slaves as it was believed to improve their strength. Garlic was also believed to ward off evil spirits, bring good luck, etc. People hung garlic in front of their homes as protection and seafarers carried garlic to prevent their ships from sinking in the sea. In medieval times garlic was considered a remedy for plague and smallpox.

Unlike other spices, garlic always had a stigma, which may have arisen due to its pungent odor. It was believed to have aphrodisiac properties and even magical powers.

Americans started warming up to garlic since the 1940s as more and more of its benefits became known. Garlic consumption in America has tripled over the past decade or so. About 20 million tons of garlic produced in the world with more than half coming out of China.

Garlic is part of the *Allium* (onion) family and is closely related to shallots, onions, Chinese onions, chives, and leeks. There are 400+ varieties of garlic in the world today.

When one thinks of garlic, the first thing that comes to mind is the smell. But beyond its sharp odor, garlic offers a number of health benefits. While most of garlic production and consumption is in Asia, garlic is finding more and more uses in the west in cooking and health supplements. China produces more than ½ of the world garlic production, close to 20 million tons. More than 90% of all garlic production in the USA comes out of California.

Most garlic bulbs are white in color and consist of 10 or more cloves. Garlic enhances the flavor of many dishes such as Indian curries, Chinese food, pizzas, and stir-fries.

The main active ingredient in garlic is called polysulphide allicin and is responsible primarily for its medicinal properties. This compound, allicin, formed when garlic cloves are chopped or crushed not only provides the medicinal properties but the distinct taste and smell as well.

Garlic is extremely nutritious and is a source of vitamins C and B6, along with the minerals manganese and selenium. Garlic also contains minor amounts of other minerals such as calcium, copper, potassium, phosphorous, and iron.

Just three cloves of garlic (about 9 grams) a day provides a recommended daily value of 8% manganese, 7 % vitamin B6, 4% vitamin C, 3% copper, 3 % selenium, and 2% each phosphorous, calcium and vitamin B1.

CLOVE

Cloves are strong, pungent and aromatic flower buds of an evergreen tree native of Indonesia and other parts of southeast Asia. Cloves have a history of centuries of use. Like nutmeg and mace, clove became popular in Europe around the 8th century. Portuguese and the Dutch occupied the Spice Islands and controlled spice trade till the 18th century. Currently cloves are cultivated in Mauritius, Madagascar, Zanzibar, and Indonesia.

Cloves can be used in gingerbread, cookies, applesauce, muffins, and cakes. Make sure they are used sparingly and in ground form in baking. Cloves are also an essential part of spice mixes such as South Asian *garam* (hot) masala, biriyani (a form of spiced rice with meat or vegetables) masala and curry powder. Additionally, cloves can be found in many different kinds of biriyani preparations.

Like many other spices, cloves also have many health benefits, including boosting the immune system, helping with digestion and stomach ulcers, liver health, regulating blood sugar, and promoting bone health. Clove contains a local anesthetic substance called eugenol and has been used in dentistry for years. A home remedy for toothache is to bite and chew a clove between the troublesome teeth.

CUMIN

Cumin originated in the Mediterranean region and was grown in Egypt and surrounding areas. It is considered one of the ancient spices and was used by Romans. There is also a mention of cumin in the Old Testament.

Today, cumin is cultivated around the world and is one of the most widely used spices. Cumin comes in the form of whole dried seeds or is ground as powder and is an integral part of Indian, Mexican, African, South Asian and other cuisines.

Cumin has many benefits and is well known for its ability to promote digestion. Cumin also helps with diabetes, improve blood cholesterol, has iron that helps with anemia, and is known to improve sleep quality. Cumin is being studied for its possible anti-cancer benefits.

FENNEL

Ancient Romans and Greeks used this native Mediterranean plant for culinary uses, as a symbol or victory or as a medicinal plant. Fennel stalks are used as a vegetable while seeds are the spice.

Fennel seeds are aromatic, sweeter, and have a flavor like aniseed or licorice. Fennel belongs to the parsley family which also includes cumin, anise and dill. Fennel is highly nutritious and has good medicinal value. It is good for indigestion, an upset stomach, flatulence and bloating. A quick home remedy for gas or flatulence is to boil water with fennel and drink the fennel water. Fennel is also known to help with respiratory problems (such as asthma), boost the immune system, and treat heartburn.

CHILI PEPPER AND CHILI POWDER

Chili peppers are, arguably, the most well-known of all the spices. Chili is a native of South and Central America and was introduced to South Asia in the 1500s by Portuguese and Spanish traders after Columbus discovered them in the Americas. There are about 25 different varieties of chili pepper, all belonging to the capsicum family and all with different "heat" levels from extremely mild to extremely hot. Today, India is the largest producer of chilies in the world.

The active ingredient contained in chili pepper is called capsaicin which gives the pungent or hot taste. Chili pepper contains anti-oxidants, vitamin C, and carotenoids that provide a number of health benefits including boosting immunity, cardiovascular health, clearing nasal and chest congestion, weight loss, and treating diabetes. Chili pepper is a key component of Indian curry powder as well as many Mexican and Asian cuisine.

CARDAMOM

Cardamom is one of the world's oldest spices. Cardamom has at least 4000 years of history. Ancient Egyptians, Greeks, and Romans used them for a variety of purposes including medicinal, perfumes, and aromatic oils. Cardamom pods were chewed to keep the breath minty and clean.

Guatemala is the leading producer of cardamom today. India and South Asian countries also produce cardamom, which is used in many Asian cuisines as a part of spice blends. Cardamom is one of the essential ingredients in almost all of the spice tea blends. Cardamom is also used in baking to enhance the flavor and aroma.

Like many other spices, cardamom is loaded with nutrients and other helpful agents that offer many health benefits from curing common colds to indigestion, lower blood pressure, improve circulation, heartburn, constipation, and many more.

BLACK PEPPER

Black pepper has a storied story among various spices. Black pepper originated from the Western Ghats of the south Indian state of Kerala. Black pepper has at least 4000 of history having been mentioned in ancient Tamil writings and in Mahabharata.

Black pepper was so valued that it was used as a form of currency. The Europeans called it black gold. Portuguese explorer Vasco De Gama discovered a trade route to India around the Cape of Good Hope as he was trying to trade spices, especially black pepper, with India's western coast. Around the same time, Christopher Columbus set sail to trade with India for black pepper and instead discovered the Americas and chili peppers.

Black pepper is currently cultivated in Vietnam, Brazil, India, and other tropical countries. Black pepper has many amazing benefits, such as preventing cancer, relieves cold and cough, improves digestion and many other benefits. Black pepper is also known for enhancing bioavailability as it enhances the absorption of nutrients in other foods we consume. For example, adding black pepper to turmeric helps curcumin absorption by 1000 times. Black pepper is used in many cuisines and is part of Indian curry powder.

CORIANDER

Coriander is also one of the oldest spices and has been in use for 5000 years. Coriander is mentioned in the Bible and Hippocrates, the ancient Greek physician, recommended coriander for medicinal uses.

Coriander is the seed cultivated from the herb cilantro or Chinese parsley. Coriander seeds have been cultivated for a long time. Coriander has several health benefits, like lowering blood sugar, decreasing blood pressure, and lowering cholesterol levels.

Coriander is usually used in conjunction with other spices and is an essential ingredient of curry powder. The amount of coriander powder used in the curry blend depends on how mild one wants the curry powder to be. The more coriander, the milder mix. Coriander leaves or cilantro is used as a seasoning herb as well.

MUSTARD SEEDS

Mustard seed is from the mustard plant, which is related to broccoli, cabbage, and Brussels sprouts. Three different varieties of mustard seeds are popular: black, brown, and yellow. Mustard seeds are a good source of selenium, magnesium, and omega-3. Mustard seeds have anti-cancer and anti-inflammatory benefits among others. Mustard seeds are crackled in oil as part of many South Asian recipes. Mustard is also used as salad dressings, rubs, and sauces.

FENUGREEK

Fenugreek is a native of the Mediterranean countries and west Asia and is part of the Fabaceae or the bean family. Fenugreek seeds are used as medicine and spice in the middle east, India, and Mediterranean. Fenugreek is considered to have benefits in treating diabetes, cholesterol, and improve blood sugar levels. Fenugreek is also believed to benefit milk production in breast-feeding, improve digestion, and reduce inflammation.

Roasted and ground fenugreek seeds are usually part of many spice mixes. Fenugreek seeds are used in cooking both fish and meat dishes. It may also be soaked in water overnight and drink the water which may help in digestion, improving cholesterol and blood sugar levels. Fenugreek leaves are used as a leafy vegetable in Indian cooking.

NUTMEG AND MACE

Nutmeg is the seed or ground spice of Myristica fragrans, an evergreen tree originally from Spice Islands. While nutmeg is the seed of this plant, the seed covering is called mace, which is considered a separate spice. Nutmeg is used in many dessert preparations such as apple and pumpkin pie, in beverages such as eggnog, chai, and coffee drinks. In cooking, both nutmeg and mace are part of curry powder, garam masala, and many Mediterranean and Middle Eastern spice mixes.

Nutmeg has a slightly twisted history than other spices. It can be toxic in large quantities. Nutmeg has hallucinogenic properties and can induce what is called nutmeg psychosis. In small quantities, nutmeg can help digestion, improve brain health, and relieve pain.

STAR ANISE

Star anise is a native of Vietnam and southwest China. The star-shaped seed from this evergreen tree is commonly used in Vietnamese and Chinese cooking and is a key ingredient in Chinese five-spice powder. Star anise considered to enhance meat flavor and is used often in spice blends for meat preparations. In the Indian subcontinent, star anise is usually part of many spice blends such as curry, garam masala, and biriyani spice mixes.

Star anise can help improve digestion and is a remedy for many digestive ailments such as bloating, gas, indigestion, and constipation.

ALLSPICE

Usually not part of Indian curry powder but used in other blends such as Ethiopian berbere and Japanese curry paste.

Allspice is the dried unripe fruit of an evergreen tree or shrub *Pimenta dioica*. Allspice was originated in the West Indies and was primarily cultivated in Jamaica. The dried fruit is spice and is considered to have a combined flavor of many spices, especially cinnamon, nutmeg, and cloves and hence it was called allspice by the English. Allspice is a key ingredient in Caribbean cuisine. Like many other spices, allspice's benefits include improving circulation, aid in digestion, and improve heart health. Allspice also has both anti-inflammatory and anti-oxidant properties.

HERBS

Rosemary

Rosemary is a herb of Mediterranean origin and is part of the mint family. It gives food a nice taste and aroma. Rosemary has anti-oxidant and anti-inflammatory properties. It is also good for brain function, improving mood, and reducing anxiety and stress among other benefits.

Basil

Basil is part of the mint family and is used in many folk and traditional medicines in Asia. There are tens of varieties of basil of which holy basil is the one that has been most researched. Like many other herbs, basil has anti-bacterial, antioxidant, and anti-inflammatory capabilities. Like rosemary, basil is also a stress and anxiety reliever. Basil also has anti-cancer properties and contains many essential oils.

Cilantro

Cilantro is the leaves of the coriander plant. Cilantro is very high in vitamin A. Cilantro helps in cleaning the body of toxic heavy metals such as mercury, arsenic, lead, cadmium, and aluminum. Cilantro has anti-oxidant, anti-inflammatory properties and offers cardiovascular benefits, restful sleep, and many others.

Thyme

Thyme boosts the immune system, is antioxidant, and helps improve circulation and protects the heart. Thyme also has anti-fungal properties and helps reduce stress.

Curry leaves

Depending on the region in South Asia, curry leaves are used as an optional flavor-enhancing ingredient. Fresh curry leaves are often fried in oil to release their aroma and flavor before sautéing onions and curry powder.

Dried curry leaves are ground and added as part of some spice mixes such as sambar or rasam powder. One can find curry leaves in Indian and Asian stores in North America and Europe. The benefits of curry leaves include helping with digestion, fighting diabetes, and lowering cholesterol.

Bay leaves

Bay leaves are most commonly used in dried form. Bay leaves are used in many Indian curries, spiced rice preparations. Bay leaves are also common in other cuisines such as French and Cuban.

Mint

Mint leaves originated in the Mediterranean region as well as in Asia. Ancient Greeks, Romans, and Indus Valley civilizations used it as an ingredient in food preparations and as a freshener for mouth and drinking water. There are more than 25 varieties of mint. Mint helps with digestion, upset stomach, and keeps the digestive system healthy. In cooking, mint is used in sauces, chutneys, rice preparations such as biriyani as well as in cooking meat.

Parsley

Parsley is known to improve immune function and reduce cancer risk. Parsley may also help in preventing diabetes and kidney stones. Parsley can be used in sauces, soups, and vegetables. Parsley is used as a key herb in middle eastern cooking.

Oregano

Like other herbs, oregano is a culinary and medicinal herb. Oregano is rich in anti-oxidants, has anti-viral and anti-inflammatory properties is considered effective in gastrointestinal (GI) disorders, respiratory tract disorders and may also help with skin conditions if used topically. Oregano is used fresh or in dried form in Greek and Italian cooking. It goes well with meats, fish and is well paired with tomatoes.

Sage

Sage is a native to the Mediterranean region. Romans believed sage has healing properties. Sage is packed with vitamin K which helps in calcium absorption. Sage has antioxidants and is also known to help improve memory and thinking. Therefore, it is potentially a good food to fight or delay Alzheimer's. In cooking, sage is known for its use in Thanksgiving meals in stuffing and turkey. Sage pairs well with fatty meats.

Saffron

Saffron is one of the costliest herbs costing upwards of $2000 per pound. Saffron is typically used in rice dishes such as pilafs, risottos, paellas, and Indian biriyani. Saffron may be used in desserts such as custards, ice creams, and cookies as well.

Lemongrass

Lemongrass is a tropical herb with a strong citrus flavor and is widely used in Chinese, Thai and Vietnamese cuisine in curries, salads, soups, and sauces. Like some of the other herbs, lemongrass is packed with anti-oxidants and has many other medicinal properties including regulating blood pressure, improving digestion, and boosting metabolism among others.

Lemongrass is seldom used in South Asian recipes but is a key ingredient for many Thai, Vietnamese, and Chinese food preparations.

CHAPTER 2. HEALTH BENEFITS OF SPICES AND HERBS

In this chapter, we examine various health benefits and medicinal properties of spices. Many of the spices have been used for over the years and are proven to be extremely safe for both their medicinal and culinary uses. They all contain excellent chemical compounds that provide benefits for many health conditions due to properties such as anti-inflammatory, antioxidant, and immune-boosting abilities. Let us examine these properties a bit closely:

ANTI-CANCER PROPERTIES

There have been more than a thousand studies conducted on the effects of curcumin, the active compound in turmeric, on cancer cells. These tests in the lab have shown that turmeric can kill or arrest the growth of cancer cells. Some studies on test animals have shown that turmeric blocked the formation of cancer-causing enzymes. Thus, turmeric could be used not only as a treatment but as prevention as well. Turmeric as part of a regular diet keeps your digestive system healthy and helps ward off colon cancer.

Many of the curcumin studies are focused on the benefits of curcumin in cancers such as colon, prostate, breast cancer and osteosarcoma.

Ginger contains the compound called 6-gingerol which is a very effective anticancer agent. 6-gingerol activates molecular mechanisms in the cancer cells that effectively destroys cells by causing them to commit suicide.

There have been many studies conducted on the effects of ginger in colorectal cancer patients that have shown the effectiveness of ginger in arresting the growth of cancer cells. This may not be surprising given how good ginger is for the gastrointestinal system. Ginger is believed to be also effective in other forms of cancer such as pancreatic cancer, ovarian cancer, and breast cancer. Further studies are required to confirm this.

Ginger's anti-nausea properties can help to treat nausea and vomiting caused by cancer treatment and chemotherapy.

There have been a number of studies conducted, especially in Asia, on the effectiveness of garlic against certain types of cancers. These studies, both population and clinical, have shown the potential benefits of garlic in the stomach, colon, pancreas, esophagus, and breast cancers.

A couple of different population studies in China have shown the reduced risk of stomach, esophagus, and prostate cancers in a population taking garlic compared to a population not taking garlic.

A study in San Francisco showed a 50% lower pancreatic cancer risk for people taking a larger amount of garlic compared to people not taking garlic or taking lower amounts.

A number of spices described in this book help reduce risks for many cancers individually and when used together can work in combination to potentially reduce the risk for a broad spectrum of cancers.

ANTI-OXIDANT PROPERTIES

Oxidative damage caused by free radicals (highly reactive molecules with unpaired electrons) contributes to the risk of cancers, heart disease, and diabetes as well as age-related macular degeneration. Free radicals tend to react with important organic substances, such as fatty acids, proteins, or DNA, causing oxidative damage.

Antioxidants help neutralize free radicals and reduce the risk of oxidative damage. They "clean up" free radicals by interacting and forming harmless substances, thereby protecting healthy cells. There are several vitamins and supplements that are known to have antioxidant properties (e.g. vitamin C & E, beta carotene, etc.). Many fruits (berries, grapes, etc.) and vegetables (kale, artichokes, bell pepper, etc.) contain antioxidants. Nuts such as walnuts and beverages such as tea and coffee also contain antioxidants. Antioxidants are often added to packaged food products to keep them from interacting with air.

Curcumin, the active ingredient in turmeric, is a potent antioxidant that can do two things: neutralize free radicals due to its chemical structure and stimulate the body's own antioxidant enzymes.

Regular garlic intake has shown to increase antioxidant enzymes in the body especially in diabetics and patients of hypertension.

Cinnamon has one of the highest levels of anti-oxidants of all spices.

Once again, anti-oxidant foods help neutralize free radicals in the body that cause oxidative cell damage and potentially cause cancer and other debilitating diseases.

ANTI-INFLAMMATORY BENEFITS

Inflammation plays an important role in the natural healing process in the human body. It helps to defend harmful invaders in our body such as bacteria that cause infection. Inflammation also helps the body carry out wound repair. Without inflammation, foreign invaders could cause damage to our bodies and ultimately kill us.

When short term, controlled inflammation is beneficial. It can become a major problem when it becomes chronic, such as arthritis. Chronic inflammation plays a major role in many serious health conditions such as heart disease, cancer, Alzheimer's, and other various degenerative conditions.

Therefore, it is very important that inflammation is contained, and chronic inflammation is fought with medicines, supplements, foods, or through a combination of all in order to reduce or prevent it from happening.

Curcumin, the main active ingredient in turmeric, has high anti-inflammatory properties and some studies have shown that it can be as good as some anti-inflammatory drugs without any side effects.

Ginger has been used for centuries as an anti-inflammatory herb. Recent studies have shown that a steady intake of ginger for a period of more than a month helped reduce inflammation in the colon. By reducing inflammation, the risk of colon cancer is also reduced. Another study has shown promise in reducing inflammation associated with osteoarthritis.

Allicin, the sulfur compound in garlic, has high anti-inflammatory properties that stimulate the body's defenses and disease-fighting capabilities and helps fight inflammation effectively.

By fighting inflammation that weakens the body's immune system and damages cells, these spices help improve the body's defenses against cancer and other major diseases.

IMMUNE SYSTEM AND INFECTIONS

A number of spices including turmeric, ginger, cinnamon, and garlic, with their antibacterial and antimicrobial properties, all have the capability to fight infections and boost the immune system. A body that is weak in its defenses against foreign invaders into the body is always at high risk for cancer and many other diseases. In addition, ginger has excellent capabilities to help maintain a healthy digestive system and stomach. A significant part of the body's immunity results from a healthy gut, and thus maintaining a healthy digestive system enhances the body's overall immunity and helps reduce the risk of not only cancer but many other diseases.

ARTHRITIS

Arthritis is a common health condition characterized by inflammation of joints. Due to its powerful anti-inflammatory characteristics, it is not surprising that turmeric can be effective in treating various kinds of arthritis. Several studies have been conducted that have shown that turmeric is effective in reducing pain, joint inflammation, and discomfort in rheumatoid arthritis (RA) which is one of the most common autoimmune diseases. Curcumin in turmeric is known to block inflammatory cytokines and enzymes. Some recent studies have shown that turmeric is effective in preventing RA as well as providing long term benefits, and some anecdotal reports have indicated that curcumin extract has been found to be highly effective in dogs with arthritis.

NEURO-PROTECTIVE

There have been multiple studies on the potential of turmeric for treating Alzheimer's and Parkinson's diseases. Much of this research is focused on antioxidant, anti-inflammatory, and anti-amyloid properties.

Though it has not been conclusively proven, there is some anecdotal evidence that turmeric could prevent the formation or even break up the amyloid-beta plaques considered to be associated with Alzheimer's disease.

Another compound in turmeric called turmerone has been shown in some studies to help create new brain cells by stimulating stem cells. This could help with arresting neurodegenerative conditions and help reduce the mental decline as people age.

Inflammation and oxidative damage to brain cells are considered the key contributing factors to the accelerated aging process. By consuming anti-oxidant and anti-inflammatory foods, one can reduce the effect of aging on the brain.

Ginger has antioxidant and anti-inflammatory properties that can help with slowing down age-related decline in brain function such as Alzheimer's disease.

Garlic is a super brain food that has great properties to help slow down aging and age-related disorders. Garlic's antioxidant and anti-inflammatory properties combined with effects in reducing cholesterol and blood pressure may help slow down brain diseases like Alzheimer's and dementia.

Cinnamaldehyde and epicatechin, two of the active compounds found in cinnamon have been studied on their effects of tau proteins that cause tangles in Alzheimer's brain. Researchers have found some evidence that these compounds in cinnamon can prevent the formation of tangles thus likely preventing or delaying Alzheimer's.

Diabetes and Alzheimer's are known to share connections similar to the heart condition and Alzheimer's. 70% of people with type 2 diabetes are known to eventually develop Alzheimer's. So, cinnamon's ability to regulate insulin levels and thus help control diabetes may also have an indirect benefit by reducing the risk of Alzheimer's.

Some studies have shown that regular intake of cinnamon helps prevent loss of neuro-protective proteins (Parkin and D-J1) that protects brain cells.

A study by the researches at Rush University Medical Center found that cinnamon can reverse the changes that occur in the brain as a result of Parkinson's. The study was conducted in mice. The study found that cinnamon is metabolized in the liver into sodium benzoate which then enters the brain and can prevent the loss of Parkin and DJ-1 proteins that protect brain cells.

Herbs such as sage have been proven to improve memory and thinking resulting in either help delay or prevent Alzheimer's.

CHOLESTEROL

Research has shown that feeding lab animals with turmeric extract resulted in reducing bad cholesterol and increasing good cholesterol, thereby reducing total cholesterol levels. In most studies, the improvements were in the 25-50% range. Curcumin's antioxidant property helps prevent oxidation of cholesterol, helps increase the metabolism of cholesterol, and reduces build-up.

Studies have shown that daily intake of ginger helps reduce LDL cholesterol (bad cholesterol). The studies were conducted on humans as well as animals. As a result, the daily use of ginger may help maintain not only a healthy gut but a healthy heart as well.

Garlic is believed to reduce both LDL (bad) cholesterol and total cholesterol. A number of research studies in humans and animals have found that the sulfur compounds in garlic help reduce LDL cholesterol and total cholesterol while they have no impact on HDL (good) cholesterol levels.

Studies have shown that daily intake of cinnamon may help reduce LDL cholesterol (bad cholesterol) and likely improve HDL cholesterol. While there is no conclusive evidence in organized studies about the benefits of cinnamon in lowering cholesterol, several anecdotal evidence and claims exist regarding cholesterol-lowering abilities of cinnamon.

PAIN

With its anti-inflammatory and antioxidant properties, it is no wonder that turmeric is an effective remedy for pain, especially joint pains as a result of inflammation or arthritis. Some studies in rats have shown that turmeric naturally activated the body's inherent pain-relieving mechanisms.

Ginger is considered to help with pain – especially exercise-induced muscle pain. Drinking some ginger juice/drink after exercise regularly may be useful to relieve muscle pain. In addition, ginger has been studied for its effectiveness for menstrual pain and cramps and has been found as effective as some of the pain medications.

Chili powder is highly effective against pain.

IMPROVED CIRCULATION

Studies have shown that curcumin has properties that help in unclogging your arteries and improving blood circulation. Turmeric could be considered a natural alternative to some of the common medications that helps prevent blood clotting. A recent study in Japan showed that curcumin improved blood circulation in a trial group the same as a group that did regular exercise.

ANTI-DEPRESSANT

Studies conducted in India comparing curcumin and Prozac have shown that it has the same effect as Prozac in managing depression and could be considered as an effective and safe alternative for cases of mild depression.

GASTROINTESTINAL BENEFITS

Studies have shown several benefits for turmeric in gastrointestinal problems. Turmeric stimulates the gallbladder to produce more bile, which helps in digestion and promotes intestinal flora. Due to its anti-inflammatory properties, several inflammatory bowel diseases such as Chron's and Ulcerative Colitis could benefit from turmeric intake. Usage of turmeric helps to heal the digestive system and supports the growth of good bacteria.

SKIN AND HAIR

Turmeric is both a powerful antioxidant and an anti-inflammatory agent, but it also has anti-bacterial and anti-microbial properties. Therefore, it is no surprise that turmeric can do wonders for your skin. Turmeric is known to help in many problems associated with skin conditions and wound healing and it has also been used in the east (especially in India) as part of beauty-enhancing skin treatments.

Pastes containing turmeric are used for treating acne, eczema, and rosacea. By applying a turmeric facial mask or paste, one can reduce skin inflammation and redness associated with eczema or rosacea skin conditions.

In some Middle Eastern countries, garlic is used as a remedy for hair loss. Fresh garlic juice or garlic oil in combination with essential oils may be applied to the scalp. There is some evidence to suggest that garlic treatment may arrest hair loss or in some cases even promote hair growth.

INDIGESTION

Ginger has been used in traditional medicine as a digestive aid for thousands of years. In the East, ginger is an essential ingredient in meat cooking not only to add flavor to the food but also to help in digestion as well. Chewing on fresh ginger or drinking ginger juice/drink can help cure minor tummy aches (due to indigestion) and help with bloating and constipation.

Ginger relieves and relaxes gastrointestinal muscles that help reduce stomach irritation. It also helps in bile production and movement of food through the gastrointestinal tract thereby helping proper metabolism and food absorption in the body.

NAUSEA AND MORNING SICKNESS

Ginger has been used as a home remedy for different forms of nausea from morning sickness and motion sickness to even nausea due to chemotherapy.

Ginger has been used for motion sickness (seasickness primarily) for centuries. Recent studies have shown that ginger is effective in preventing both morning sickness and pregnancy-related nausea.

DIABETES AND HEART HEALTH

Ginger is believed to have several properties that help in maintaining a healthy heart including blood thinning, stimulating circulation, reducing cholesterol levels, and preventing heart attacks and strokes.

A study conducted on gingerol's effect on blood sugar found that there were significant benefits to using ginger powder in lowering blood sugar levels in diabetic patients.

One of the active ingredients in cinnamon, hydroxychalcone is believed to help increase insulin sensitivity and help promote insulin uptake into the cells.

One of the flavonoids found in cinnamon called proanthocyanin, is considered to penetrate cells and help in maintaining insulin balance within the cells.

Cinnamon is known to have a positive influence on the digestive enzymes in the stomach. Cinnamon helps in slowing down the breakdown of carbohydrates and thus regulate post-meal insulin levels.

These are all extremely beneficial properties of cinnamon in countering diabetic conditions. Numerous studies have confirmed the anti-diabetic effects of cinnamon.

As we all know cinnamon has a natural sweet taste and therefore is a great ingredient for baking and in the preparation of desserts. The sweetness helps even as a mild substitute for sugar (for example in yogurts, teas etc.) that not only act as a sugar substitute but also provide tremendous benefit for people with diabetes.

LOWER BLOOD PRESSURE

Elevated blood pressure or hypertension is one of the key contributors to heart diseases such as heart attacks and strokes.

A number of studies in humans have found that daily intake of garlic has very beneficial effects in lowering hypertension. In some studies, these benefits were as good as prescription medications.

IMPROVED PHYSICAL PERFORMANCE

Egyptians, Greeks and Romans used to feed garlic to their warriors as well as slaves in hopes of improving their performance in the war or their slave output. Ancient Greeks fed garlic to Olympic athletes believing that garlic improved their physical capabilities, helping them win competitions.

Garlic could be considered one of the earliest performance-enhancing substances.

COLD AND FLU

Allicin, the sulfur compound found in garlic has anti-microbial, anti-fungal and anti-virus capabilities. As a result, garlic can help fight a number of common ailments that rise out of bacteria, fungal, or viral infections.

In several studies conducted on the effectiveness of garlic, regular consumption of garlic has been found to be effective in 1) preventing cold and flu and 2) speedy recovery in cases where the subjects of the study did catch a cold.

Many other spices such as chili and turmeric also help fight common cold symptoms. Ginger tea is a good remedy for cold.

BONE HEALTH

Garlic contains a number of minerals and vitamins that are considered the foundation for bone health such as zinc, manganese, Vitamin-B6, and Vitamin-C. In addition, regular use of garlic can increase estrogen in females helping to fight bone loss and osteoarthritis.

ANTIBACTERIAL AND ANTI-PARASITIC

Allicin, the active ingredient in garlic, is an extremely anti-bacterial and anti-parasitic compound. Allicin protects the garlic plant from fungus, bacteria, and parasites while growing in the soil. This property of allicin is also effective in humans when consumed. There has been a lot of evidence of garlic helping to fight common infections such as cold, flu, ear infection, etc. This is one of the reasons garlic was used as a remedy for plague and smallpox during medieval times.

DETOX AGENT

Garlic with its anti-fungal, anti-bacterial, and anti-parasitic properties is a very good detox agent for the body. In addition, allicin, the sulfur compound in garlic, can neutralize heavy metals, especially neutralizing lead toxicity in the body.

CHAPTER 3. SPICE MIXES

ORIGIN

Spice blends were used in cooking by many civilizations including Greek, Roman, Egyptian, and Indus Valley Civilizations. They mixed and matched these spices in the preparation of food. Mostly, these spices were used to enhance food flavor or to increase the shelf life of the prepared food as no refrigeration or another modern food preservation was available. Over time, these ancient civilizations recognized that these spice blends have health benefits beyond flavoring or preserving food.

CURRY POWDER

While the use of spice blends dates 4000 years ago, the idea of "curry" powder came from the 18[th]century English colonists who were part of the South Asian spice trade. English did not quite understand the local population's preparation and use of spice blends. They called anything prepared using a spice blend, "curry".

The word "curry" originated from the word "kari" which means "sauce or relish for rice" in Tamil, a language spoken in the southern part of India, Srilanka, and parts of southeast Asia.

Curry is usually an Indian dish made of meat, fish or vegetables cooked with spices and herbs. The end product is that the cooked meat, fish, or vegetables are fully soaked in a savory spicy sauce. Curry is usually eaten with rice or bread. The dish is very colorful – most often red or yellow and in some cases, green.

Curry powder or Indian curry powder is a mix of several spices, in some cases up to 20 different spices and herbs. The most notable spices used are coriander, cumin, turmeric, and chili powder. Other ingredients may include cardamom, cinnamon, black pepper, ground ginger, ground mustard, fenugreek, nutmeg, and fennel. By varying the proportion of these spices, one can create mild, medium, or hot curry powder with distinct taste differences as well as health benefits.

Besides Indian curry, there are many other variants of curry from other countries such as Japanese curry, Thai curry, Ethiopian curry, and many others.

The spices and herbs used in curry are known for many health benefits including anti-cancer, anti-inflammatory, antioxidant, and many others. Curry, therefore, is an excellent health food and should be incorporated into your food habits and diet regime.

One can make their own curry powder by mixing various spice powders or blending various whole spices. This offers a lot of flexibility in terms of controlling the spice and heat level as well as going with the spices one likes or more beneficial and avoid or limit others. Many recipes for making spice blends for curry powder are included in this book.

If one wants to go for pre-packaged curry powders or curry paste, there are many options available on the market. You may want to choose carefully as no two recipes for the packaged curry powder are the same. Pre-packaged curry powder and paste are available in many South Asian and Indian stores as well as online stores such as Amazon.

Variations of Indian curry powder

While curry powder is a more generic form of spice blend, there are several variations available in the market.

Regular curry powder contains more turmeric, coriander, and cumin and is more yellow in color.

Madras curry powder is typically a spicier version and contains more chili powder (therefore redder in color) in the blend.

Hot curry powder, like Madras curry powder, has extra kick due to the added chili powder or hotter version of the chili used in addition to ginger powder.

Maharaja curry powder is rich, mild, and sweet and perfumed by the use of saffron and cardamom.

Sweet curry powder is the mildest and maybe the right spice mix for someone who is starting with curry powder. Sweet curry powder contains less chili, more turmeric, and other mild spices.

MORE SOUTH ASIAN SPICE MIXES

Garam Masala

Garam Masala, which literally means "hot spice", is a spice mix of north Indian origin. It is not considered curry powder, but sometimes is used along with curry powder or occasionally used as a substitute. Garam masala typically includes coriander, cumin, cinnamon, nutmeg, cloves, and peppercorns among other things. Garam masala has a bit more pungent flavor than curry powder.

Sambhar powder

Sambhar (or Saambaar, Saambar) is a lentil-based stew or soup cooked in tamarind broth and seasoned with Sambhar powder. This is a popular dish in the south of India and Srilanka. Sambhar is eaten as a soup or with south Indian dishes such as idli (steamed rice cake) or dosa (lentil crepes) or just plain cooked rice. As with curry powder, there are many variations of Sambhar masala you can buy on the market. There are many variations in the preparation of Sambhar dish as well.

Biriyani masala

Biriyani masala is not strictly used to make curries but is a spice mix for making seasoned rice mixed with meat (chicken, mutton, beef, prawn or fish) or vegetables. Biriyani masala also comes in many varieties and often indicative of the locality or origin of the dish. The spice mixes as well as the mode of preparation, vary according to the place it originated (e.g. Hyderabadi, Malabar, Bombay, Karachi) as well the type of meat or vegetable used.

Rasam powder

Rasam is a South Indian soup (similar to Sambhar but much lighter and thinner) that is based on tamarind or tomato and seasoned with black pepper, cumin, chili powder, and other seasonings. It is typically eaten with cooked rice or most often as a spicy soup that is well known as a remedy to clear a stuffy nose, mild headache, and flu symptoms.

Chaat masala

Chaat masala (or chat masala) is a mild spice mix consisting of dried mango powder, cumin, black pepper, coriander, and dried ginger (and some other spices depending on taste). It is originated in South Asia and is usually sprinkled on fruits, toasts, and salads. The chaat masala is also sprinkled on snacks sold by vendors on the streets of Mumbai, Delhi, and other north Indian (primarily) cities.

Vindaloo masala

Vindaloo is a type of curry but is distinguished as Portuguese influenced cuisine from the state of Goa in India. In a traditional Goan cuisine, the meat is usually marinated in vinegar, ginger, garlic, and other spices overnight before cooking. Vindaloo masala typically contains red chilies, cumin, cinnamon, cardamom, cloves, black pepper, tomato paste and/or vinegar.

Curry paste

Curry paste is an alternative to curry powder. Curry paste is made by grinding the curry masala or ingredients into a paste form. Curry masala usually includes fresh ginger instead of ginger powder, fresh garlic and at times tomato puree or paste and shallots or red onions. In some cases, vinegar is added to make it a paste. Most often the curry paste is fried in oil to make sure the spices, onions, tomatoes, and other ingredients are cooked and cured. Frying the curry paste in oil enhances its flavor and also increases its shelf life.

CHINESE, JAPANESE AND THAI SPICE MIXES

Japanese Curry mix/paste

Curry became a popular dish in Japan after the British introduced it in the 19th century. Japanese adapted the Indian curry and it became one of Japan's national dishes.

Japanese curry powder is a mild version of Indian curry powder. However, the preparation of Japanese curry is quite different than that of Indian curry. Japanese curry is not usually very spicy but is a bit sweet and savory in taste and thick in texture. While you can use a mild version of curry spice recipe in this book to make Japanese curry (rice), there are a number of Japanese curry blends are available in the market such as Vermont curry, Java curry, and Torokeru curry.

Thai Curry mix/paste

Thai curry refers to dishes made with Thai curry paste. Thai curry can be made with meat, seafood, vegetables, or tofu. One of my all-time favorite Thai dishes is roasted duck curry. Thai curry paste differs from Indian curry powder or paste due to the type of ingredients added. The typical ingredients in Thai curry paste include red chilies, coriander, onions/shallots, lemongrass, lime, shrimp paste, fish sauce, garlic, and ginger or galangal. Ingredients such as turmeric, cumin, black pepper, cardamom, and others may be added depending on the main ingredient for the curry dish – such as meat, seafood, or vegetables. Many of the Thai curry dishes use coconut milk as the base.

Thai curry comes in 3 distinct flavors, Thai red curry, Thai yellow curry, and Thai green curry.

Thai red curry is medium spicy and has a citrus flavor by adding lemongrass, lime peel, and galangal besides other ingredients.

Thai yellow curry is less spicy than the red curry and contains more turmeric that gives it the yellow color

Thai green curry contains cilantro and Jalapenos instead of chili powder

Chinese Five Spice

Chine five spice is a mixture of five spices – cinnamon, cloves, black peppercorns, fennel, and star anise. These five spices a bit of sweet, savory, bitter, and sour tastes. The Chinese five-spice goes with meat, vegetables, and baked food.

Gomasio

Gomasio is a Japanese condiment made of ground toasted sesame seeds mixed with coarse salt. Gomasio can be sprinkled on top of rice, steamed edamame, salads or noodles.

Togarashi

Togarashi is a Japanese spice blend consisting of 7-8 spices including ginger, garlic, sesame seeds, poppy seeds, hemp seeds, seaweed, citrus peel, and chilies. This mix may be used within cooking meat, soups, and vegetables. The typical use is to sprinkle it over noodles, salads, tempuras, steamed vegetables, steamed rice, or fries.

AFRICAN AND MIDDLE EASTERN SPICE MIXES

Ethiopian Berbere Mix

Berbere is a spice mix used to make many Ethiopian dishes such as *doro wat* (chicken) and *misir wat* (split lentil). Berbere mix usually consists of chili powder, coriander, nutmeg, allspice, cinnamon, cloves, fenugreek, garlic, ginger, and onion powder.

Dukkah

Dukkah is an Egyptian spice and nut mix. The blend includes hazelnuts, sesame seeds, cumin, black pepper, coriander, and salt. The ingredients are roasted and ground in a food processor. Dukkah may be used to top vegetables, stir into pasta dishes, and also used for toasting bread topped with olive oil and dukkah powder.

Harissa Seasoning

Harissa seasoning is from Tunisia, Morocco, and other North African countries. Made with roasted chilies (main ingredient), coriander, garlic, cumin, and caraway seeds. The ingredients are ground and combined with tomato paste and lemon juice to make a harissa paste. Harissa paste may be used as a dip, mixed while making burgers or used to cook chicken.

Ras el Hanout

Ras el Hanout is a spice blend with a number of spices such as cardamom, clove, cinnamon, coriander, paprika, mace, nutmeg, peppercorn, and turmeric

Advieh

Advieh is a Persian mix of spices and dried rose petals. Spices include cardamom, cinnamon, cloves, nutmeg, and cumin. Advieh blend is used in stews, rice, and meat dishes.

Baharat

Baharat is a middle eastern spice blend similar to Indian garam masala and is used in cooking meat, fish, chicken, and rice. Baharat typically includes peppercorns, coriander, allspice, paprika, cumin, cardamom, cinnamon, cloves, and nutmeg.

AMERICAS AND EUROPEAN SPICE MIXES

Khmeli Suneli

Khmeli suneli is a Georgian mix consisting of fenugreek seeds and leaves, summer savory, black peppercorns, and coriander. This spice blend can be used with soups, meat, and also vegetables.

Fines Herbes

Fines Herbes is a French blend of herbs such as chives, parsley, tarragon, and chervil. The blend is used for salad topping or to season dishes at the end of cooking.

Barbeque Rub or Dry Rub

Distinctly American, barbeque rub or dry rub usually contains cayenne pepper, paprika, cumin, black pepper, garlic, onion powder, mustard powder. salt and brown sugar. Originally from Kansas City, this blend is pretty popular for barbequing all over the US.

Jerk Spice

Jerk spice is a Jamaican mixture that typically includes allspice, chili, black pepper, cinnamon, and thyme.

Pumpkin Spice
Pumpkin spice is also from North America is made with spices such as cinnamon, nutmeg, ginger, and cloves. This blend is not just for pumpkin pie but also used for ice cream, yogurt, and morning lattes.

Adobo
From Latin America, adobo is an all-purpose seasoning that contains garlic, oregano, and black pepper among other spices.

OTHER SPICE MIXES

There are a number of other mixes available on the market. These may not have the same history as curry powder or other spice mixes, but they are worth mentioning here:

- Fajita seasoning
- Cajun spice mix
- Chili seasoning
- Herbes De Provence
- Indian chili and lentil chutney powder
- Taco seasoning
- Poultry seasoning
- Za'atar
- Kohlapuri Masala

- Panch Phoron

Many of these spice mixes are specific to different regions and have been used over time in the regional cuisine. These spice mixes vary in their spice level and complexity from mild seasoning mix to more complex and spicy mixes that need to be tempered and cooked to bring out the flavor or to make it palatable.

If you like to experiment with spices, the possibilities are endless. Once you understand the basic characteristics of the spice or herb, you can use your imagination to create the blend that you like by varying the proportion of the ingredients and the swapping in and out the ingredients itself.

CHAPTER 4. TIPS FOR COOKING WITH SPICES

This chapter discusses general tips and recommendations on cooking and using spices. As we have discussed extensively in previous chapters, spices and herbs broadly provide the many benefits.

- Color your food and make it attractive to eat
- Provide flavor and taste to the food without adding unhealthy components like salt and fat
- Transforms even ordinary/common food into tasty dishes saving money
- Spices and herbs make the cooked food healthier by preventing the formation of harmful compounds during cooking
- Spices and herbs are a very good source of micro-nutrients such as anti-oxidants, anti-inflammatory compounds, vitamins and minerals
- Stimulates appetite, improve digestion and help maintain a healthy intestine which in turn improves immunity and general health
- Protects from many health conditions such as cancer, diabetes, and cholesterol, etc.
- Helps in reversing some diseases
- Boosts brain function and slow down the aging process

Below are the suggestions when you are starting out cooking with and using spices and herbs:

1. Test if you can tolerate a specific spice

Test out spices to determine if you are allergic to any of the spices or you simply don't like any. This can be done by trying out these spices in small amounts either in cooking or in drinks. You may be allergic to some spices and it can cause serious issues. Once, a friend of mine offered masala chai (spiced tea) to his landlord only to have him a serious reaction and had to call emergency medical services.

2. Try out spices individually first before trying various spice blends

Individual spices offer many benefits and also can be simple to use when you are starting out experimenting with spices. Ginger and garlic may be used with any meat dish. Turmeric similarly can be used while sautéing onions and can color your vegetables and make it more palatable.

3. Start with the mild spices or spices you have already been exposed to. I recommend the following order:

   a. Cinnamon. You might already have been using this and is ok as part of desserts or baked foods
   b. Black Pepper. Black pepper is also part of some of the common foods that you eat on a

daily basis including soups, pasta, burgers, etc.

c. Chili powder
d. Turmeric powder
e. Coriander Powder
f. Cumin
g. Fennel
h. Other spices

The reason for this suggested order is for you to start with some of the spices you may already have been exposed through foods from some of the popular restaurants and frozen foods from supermarkets.

4. Do you need to temper the spice mix?

Tempering, blooming or gently frying spices achieves the following:

a. It reduces the pungent or raw taste of the spices
b. It deepens flavor
c. It helps the body in easy absorption of the micro-nutrients in the spices. For example, curcumin in turmeric is not easily absorbed. But tempering them in oil makes it much easier for the body to absorb.
d. Tempering is required/recommended for pungent spices such as chili, coriander, cumin, etc. but spices like cardamom, cinnamon, nutmeg, and ginger may be used directly such as done in spice tea or baking

5. How to temper or fry spices

Method 1:

    a. Add 2-3 teaspoons of butter, vegetable oil, coconut oil, or olive oil to a sauté pan or instant pot set in sauté mode. Make sure the heat is set to medium so as not to burn the spice

    b. Test out the heat of the pan by dropping a bit of spice. If it bubbles up and simmers the pan is ready. If not, turn up the heat a bit more

    c. Add the spices all together and stir well so it is coated with oil. Stir for a minute so the spices are fried, and aroma is released. Now you can add vegetables or meat and cook.

Method 2: Tempering spice with onions, garlic and/ or ginger

    d. Add 2-3 teaspoons of butter, vegetable oil, coconut oil or olive oil to a sauté pan or instant pot set in sauté mode.

    e. Add onions (and ginger and garlic), stir well until onions turn translucent

    f. Add the spices all together and stir well so it is coated with oil. Stir for a minute so the spices are fried, and aroma is released. Now you can add vegetables or meat and cook.

Method 3: Tempering spice paste

An alternative way to fry spice is to make it a paste first and then fry it in oil as described in 6. The easy way to make the spice mix into a paste is to add one tablespoon or enough water to spice and mix it to make a past.

6. Other general tips for using or cooking with spices

- Add ½ -1 teaspoon of turmeric powder and a pinch of black pepper powder when sautéing onions, herbs, or vegetables.

- Sauté crushed garlic and ginger in oil first before sautéing veggies or meats.

- Add a small piece of ginger/ turmeric root or both to the blender while making the smoothie.

- Make marinades using a combination of turmeric, chili, coriander and cumin powders with yogurt and ginger-garlic paste

- Make your own curry powder – by mixing one-part turmeric, one-part chili powder, one-part coriander powder, and optional roasted and ground fenugreek, cumin, and mustard seeds.

- Sauté ½-1 teaspoon turmeric powder and a pinch of black pepper powder while making your favorite soup.

- Pickle garlic in vinegar.

- Roast garlic and use it to top salads.

- Use garlic oil for sautéing

- Add ginger, cardamom, cinnamon nutmeg or fennel powder or a combination of these while baking.

- Add ginger paste (or ginger-garlic paste) to your marinades for grilling meat or fish.

- Add fresh ginger, cardamom, and cinnamon individually or in combination in making tea.

- Chew a piece of raw ginger (good for an upset stomach and nausea).

- Add 1-2 cloves of garlic to the blender while making a smoothie.

- Sprinkle mild herb and spice mixes on top of salads, pasta, rice or other dishes to enhance the flavor

- Cinnamon, cardamom, fennel, and nutmeg are *sweet* spices. These may be used individually or in combination in baking, smoothies, teas, and other sweet recipes. All these spices go well with rice preparations as well.

CHAPTER 5. COOKING VEGAN WITH SPICES

Seasoning or cooking vegan food with spices and herbs provides immense benefits – not only of a plant-based lifestyle but also due to many health benefits and disease-fighting properties of spices and herbs. These spices and herbs transform some of the bland veggies into yummy food. Below are some of the suggestions and recipes.

LEAFY GREENS

There are many dishes one can make with leafy greens by itself or combining with vegetables (such as potatoes, mushrooms, corn. Garbanzo beans, lentils), cheese (Indian cottage cheese), or meat (chicken). I have included a couple of recipes here just to demonstrate the use of spices with leafy greens. You can find many other recipes or on the internet or just use your imagination to try to come up with a totally new one.

Spices & herbs that go with it:

- Mustard seeds (whole)
- Cumin seeds (whole or powder)
- Turmeric (powder)
- Garlic (crushed or chopped)
- Ginger (grated)
- Ginger-garlic paste
- Green chilies, Jalapenos
- Chili powder

- Black pepper powder
- Cayenne pepper
- Cilantro
- Mint
- Herb mixes and mild spice mixes may be used to top steamed leafy greens

SPINACH / RED CHARD

Ingredients

- 2 tsp coconut oil (olive oil or vegetable oil can be used as well)
- 1 bunch of fresh spinach or red chard washed and chopped or 1 lb. bag of fresh spinach
- 1 tsp cumin seeds
- ½ tsp turmeric powder
- ¼ tsp black pepper powder
- 1 medium onion chopped
- 3 cloves of garlic crushed

Method

1. In a pan, heat oil, crackle cumin seeds. Add onions, crushed garlic. Sauté till onions become translucent.
2. Add rest of turmeric powder, and pepper powder and mix well.
3. Now add the spinach, mix well and cook covered medium heat for about 1-2 minutes or until it starts simmering (there will be enough water from spinach for it to simmer)
4. Reduce heat to low and cook covered for about 4-5 minutes stirring in between.

Recipe Notes:

1. This recipe may be adapted for most leafy greens such as collard greens, dandelion greens, beets leaves, or even cabbage. Greens like Kale is not suitable for this recipe

2. If you like more heat, you can add ¼ - ½ tsp chili powder along with the rest of the spices. Also, green chili or Jalapeno may be added along with onions and garlic.

3. You can add heavy cream and/or grated cheese once the spinach is cooked

4. If you are using mustard seeds, crackle them along with cumin seeds before adding onions

5. If you like coconut, grated coconut may be added once the spinach is cooked most of the water content is evaporated.

SPINACH AND POTATO

Basic Ingredients

- 2 cups of potatoes peeled and cut into 1-inch cubes
- 4 cups of spinach washed and chopped
- 2 tsp coconut or olive oil
- ½ tsp cumin seeds
- ¼ tsp black pepper powder
- 1 medium onion chopped
- ½ tsp turmeric
- Salt to taste
- ¼ tsp chili powder

- 2 green chilies seeds removed and chopped
- 2 cloves of garlic crushed
- Vegetable/Chicken/Bone broth – 1/2 cup

Method

1. Heat oil in a pan. Add oil and crackle cumin seeds
2. Add garlic and green chilies, mix and then add onions. Sauté until onions are golden brown.
3. Add turmeric, chili powder, and stir for 1-2 minutes.
4. Add potatoes mix well for about 2-3 minutes so potatoes are coated with spices. Add vegetable broth/chicken broth/bone broth
5. Close the lid and cook for 3-4 minutes or until potatoes are tender.
6. Now add the spinach and keep stirring for about 2-3 minutes or until spinach gets cooked

Switch off heat, serve with bread, naan or rice

Recipe Notes:

1. An alternative (and maybe faster) way to make this recipe is to use pre-boiled, peeled, and cubed pieces of potatoes. In this case, potatoes and spinach may be added together and let spinach cook while potatoes become more tender and absorb flavor.

LENTILS & BEANS

There are probably a hundred recipes for cooking various lentils with different spices. Some of the famous Indian dishes such as *daal, sambhar, rasam* uses lentils, and a generous amount of spices. Based on the kind of lentils used the spices added, and other vegetables used in combination, a number of different lentil-based dishes may be prepared. Lentils and beans may be cooked in dry form (without much sauce), or curry (with some sauce) or soup (sambhar, rasam)

SPICY CHICKPEAS

Basic Ingredients

- 2 cans of chickpeas drained and washed
- 2 tsp coconut or olive oil
- ¼ tsp black pepper powder
- 1 medium onion sliced
- 1 tsp turmeric
- 2 medium tomato chopped
- Salt to taste
- ¼ cup cilantro chopped
- Vegetable broth – 1/2 cup

Optional Ingredients
- ½ tsp cumin seeds
- 1-2 jalapenos sliced (seed out/in)
- 2-3 cloves of garlic crushed
- ½ inch ginger chopped into fine pieces
- ½-1 tsp curry powder

Method

1. Heat oil in a pan and crackle optional cumin seeds
2. Add onions, optional garlic, ginger, and jalapenos; sauté until onions are golden brown.
3. Add turmeric, pepper, and optional curry powder and stir for 1-2 minutes.

4. Add chopped tomatoes and mix well and then add vegetable broth
5. Add chickpeas and mix well
6. Close and cook for about 5 minutes or until the tomatoes are tender, add the cilantro and salt.

Mix well and serve hot as a side dish with rice or bread.

Recipe Notes

1. There are many optional ingredients listed, one could use all of them or pick and choose based on your taste.
2. The jalapenos vary in their heat level. If you choose to use them, you can take seeds out to reduce the heat. This note applies to all the recipes in this book.

SPICY LENTILS AND KALE

Basic Ingredients

- 1 cup split red lentil washed and soaked
- 2 tsp coconut or olive oil
- ¼ tsp black pepper powder
- 1 medium onion sliced
- 1 tsp turmeric
- 2 medium tomato chopped
- 1 bunch of kale washed and chopped.
- Salt to taste
- ¼ cup cilantro chopped
- Vegetable/bone broth – 2 cups

Optional Ingredients
- ½ tsp cumin seeds

- 1-2 jalapenos sliced (seed out/in)
- 2-3 cloves of garlic crushed
- ½ inch ginger chopped into fine pieces
- ½-1 tsp curry powder

Method

1. Cook lentils, chopped kale, and tomatoes together in a pressure cooker or instant pot. Set the instant pot to lentils or in manual setting cook for about 15-20 minutes in high pressure
2. Heat oil in a pan and crackle optional cumin seeds
3. Add onions, optional garlic, ginger, and jalapenos; sauté until onions are golden brown.
4. Add turmeric, pepper, and optional curry powder and stir for 1-2 minutes.
5. Add cooked lentils and kale. Mix well
6. Simmer for about 2-3 minutes, add the cilantro and salt.

Mix well and serve hot as a side dish with rice or bread.

Recipe Notes:

1. Instead of kale any of the leafy vegetables may be used.
2. Instead of leafy beans or in addition to leafy beans, one may add other vegetables such as carrot, cabbage tec.

VEGETABLES

CAULIFLOWER AND POTATO

Basic Ingredients

- 2 medium potatoes peeled and cut into 1-inch cubes
- ½ head of cauliflower washed and cut into pieces (same size as potato)
- 2 tsp oil
- ¼ tsp black pepper powder
- 1 medium onion sliced
- 1 tsp turmeric
- 1-2 medium tomato chopped
- Salt to taste
- ¼ cup cilantro chopped
- Vegetable/bone broth – 1 cup

Optional Ingredients
- ½ tsp cumin seeds
- 1-2 jalapenos sliced (seed out/in)
- 2-3 cloves of garlic crushed
- ½ inch ginger chopped into fine pieces
- ½-1 tsp curry powder

Method

1. Add oil in pan and crackle optional cumin seeds
2. Add onions, optional garlic, ginger, and jalapenos; sauté until onions are golden brown.
3. Add turmeric, pepper, and optional curry powder and stir for 1-2 minutes.
4. Add chopped tomatoes, potatoes and cauliflower, mix well and then add vegetable broth

5. Close the lid and cook on low-medium heat about 10-15 minutes or until both potatoes and cauliflower are cooked.
6. Switch off heat, add the cilantro and salt.

Mix well and serve hot as a side dish with rice or bread.

Recipe Note

1. As with earlier recipes the optional ingredients allow you to pick and choose the ones you like and how much creative you want to be with this recipe.

SPICY MASHED POTATO

Basic Ingredients

- 5 medium potatoes washed
- 2 tsp oil
- 1 medium onion sliced
- 1 tsp turmeric
- 3-4 medium tomato chopped
- Salt to taste
- ¼ cup cilantro chopped
- Vegetable broth – 1/2 cup

Optional Ingredients
- ½ tsp cumin seeds
- 1-2 jalapenos sliced (seed out/in)
- 2-3 cloves of garlic crushed
- ½ inch ginger chopped into fine pieces

Method

1. Boil water in a large pot. Add potatoes and salt. Cook until potatoes are tender. Drain and peel potatoes once cooled down and mash potatoes using a potato masher and set aside
2. Add oil in a pan and crackle optional cumin seeds
3. Add onions, optional garlic, ginger, and jalapenos; sauté until onions are golden brown.
4. Add turmeric and stir for 1 minute
5. Add chopped tomatoes. Mix and cook for a 1-2 minutes
6. Add mashed potato and mix well
7. Switch off heat, add the cilantro and salt to taste.

This goes well with naan or bread

SPICY STEAMED BROCCOLI

Basic Ingredients

- 1 lb. broccoli florets washed
- 2 tsp oil
- 1 medium onion sliced
- 1 tsp turmeric
- Salt to taste
- ¼ cup cilantro chopped
- 1-2 jalapenos sliced seed in
- 1 tbsp medium-hot salsa
- ½ tsp mustard seeds (optional)
- 2-3 cloves of garlic crushed (optional)
- ¼ cup vegetable/bone broth

Method

1. Add oil and crackle optional mustard seeds
2. Add onions, optional garlic, and jalapenos; sauté until onions are golden brown.
3. Add turmeric and stir for 1-2 minutes. Add salsa.
4. Add broccoli florets mix well so that it is coated with the spices. add vegetable broth
5. Close the lid and cook or 15 minutes or until done in low-medium heat.
6. Switch off heat, add the cilantro and salt.

Mix well and serve hot as a side dish with rice or bread.

Eggplant Curry

Basic Ingredients

- 2 medium eggplants
- 2 tsp oil
- 1 medium onion sliced
- 1 tsp turmeric
- ½ tsp garam masala
- 2-3 medium tomatoes chopped
- Salt to taste
- ¼ cup cilantro chopped
- 1 tsp lemon juice

Optional Ingredients
- ½ tsp cumin seeds
- 1-2 jalapenos sliced (seed out/in)
- 2-3 cloves of garlic crushed
- ½ inch ginger chopped into fine pieces
- ½-1 tsp curry powder

Method

1. Roast the eggplants in the oven set to 400 degrees for about 10 minutes. Make sure that the skin is charred slightly and easily peelable.
2. Remove the peels from the eggplant. Mash the meat and set it aside.
3. Add oil and crackle optional cumin seeds
4. Add onions, optional garlic, ginger, and jalapenos; sauté until onions are golden brown.
5. Add turmeric, garam masala, and optional curry powder and stir for 1-2 minutes.
6. Add chopped tomatoes, mix well and add mashed eggplant.
7. Close the lid and cook for about 10 minutes in medium setting.
8. Switch off heat, add lemon juice the cilantro and salt. Mix well and serve hot as a side dish with rice or bread.

Recipe Note

1. There are many optional ingredients listed, one could use all of them or pick and choose based on your taste.

CHAPTER 6. FISH AND MEAT DISHES

FISH

There are many different recipes for cooking fish with spices depending on the region the recipe originated from, type of fish, locally available spices, and the individual taste or the kinds of other ingredients used. The following individual spices or a combination go well with spiced fish preparations:

Spices & herbs that go with it:

- Mustard seeds (whole)
- Turmeric (powder)
- Coriander (powder)
- Cumin (powder)
- Fenugreek
- Garlic
- Ginger
- Chili (chopped green chilies or powder)
- Black pepper
- Cayenne pepper
- Curry leaves
- Curry powder or garam masala

10 MINUTE SALMON CURRY

Ingredients

- Skinless Salmon 1lb. Cleaned and cut in 2-inch pieces
- 1 tsp chili powder

- 1 tsp coriander powder
- Black pepper powder- ¼ tsp
- 1 medium onion
- Grated ginger 2 tsp
- Crushed garlic 4-5 cloves
- Curry leaves-2 sprigs (optional)
- 1 cup medium salsa or picante sauce

Method

1. Combine all the spices powders – chili, turmeric, coriander, and pepper powder together in a bowl. Add 2 tsp or just enough water to make a thick paste and set aside.
2. Heat oil in a pan add ginger, garlic, onions, optional green chilies, and curry leaves. Sauté until onion becomes translucent.
3. Add the masala paste and mix well on low flame (Wet the masala to make sure it gets fried but not burnt).
4. After about 30 seconds (once masala gets fried), add salsa and mix. Now add salmon pieces. Gently mix so the salmon pieces are covered in the sauce, but the salmon is not broken. Cover and cook for 5 minutes.

This is a quick way to make salmon. The salsa or picante sauce gives the acidity and the spices give the heat and it is super easy. Goes with rice or bread.

Recipe Notes:

1. This recipe may also be used to make fish curry from canned tuna, sardine, or any other canned fish.

Follow the same recipe and you will get yummy fish curry out of bland canned fish in no time.

2. Chopped Jalapenos may be added for additional heat.

SALMON WITH GREEN MANGO

Ingredients

- Skinless Salmon 2lb. Cleaned and cut in 2-inch pieces
- Chili powder 1-4 tsp (depending on your tolerance level)
- turmeric 1 tsp
- Coriander powder- 1 tbsp
- Fenugreek powder-1/4 tsp or fenugreek seeds ½ tsp
- Black pepper powder- ¼ tsp
- Mustard seeds-1/2 tsp
- 1 medium onion
- Grated ginger 2 tsp
- Crushed garlic 4-5 cloves
- Curry leaves-2 sprigs (optional)
- Washed and cut green mango (with skin or skin removed depending on your preference) – 2 cups
- Water-1 to 1.5 cups(or as required)
- Salt to taste
- 2-4 sliced green chilies or jalapeños, seeds removed (optional)

Method

1. Combine all the spices powders – chili, turmeric, coriander, fenugreek, and pepper powder together in

a bowl. Add 2 tsp or just enough water to make a thick paste and set aside.

2. Heat oil in a pan and splutter mustard seeds and fenugreek (if seeds used instead of powder).

3. Add ginger, garlic, onions, optional green chilies, and curry leaves. Sauté until onion becomes translucent.

4. Add the masala paste and mix well on low flame (Wet the masala to make sure it gets fried but not burnt).

5. After about 30 seconds (once masala gets fried), add about 2 cups of water mix and then add the cut mango pieces.

6. Cover it and bring it a boil on medium heat. Now add individual fish pieces into the pan.

7. Mix gently, making sure the fish pieces are not broken up and that all the pieces are coated with the gravy

8. Cover the pan and cook it for about 20 minutes or until fish is done and the gravy is thick. Switch off the flame and keep it covered for 30 minutes for the fish to soak in the spices and mango flavor.

Serve with rice or bread.

Notes:

1. Paprika may be used instead of chili powder if you desire to make it less spicy.

2. Any other fish may be used instead of salmon.

3. Instead of mango, tamarind or Garcinia Cambogia (the scientific name for black tamarind available in Asian stores) may be used.

4. Green chilies or jalapeños add more heat to the fish curry. Use it depending on your taste.

FISH FRY

Below is a recipe for fish stakes marinated with spices and then shallow fried. This could be eaten as an appetizer and also served with rice. Fish stakes with bones removed or fishes with larger or easy to remove bones are ideal. Salmon, Tilapia, catfish filets, pomfret or kingfish may be used.

Ingredients

- 1 lb. fish stakes
- 1 tbsp chili powder
- ¼ tsp black pepper powder
- ¼ tsp turmeric powder
- 1 tbsp ginger garlic paste
- 1tsp lime juice

Method

1. Combine all the spices powders, salt, ginger garlic paste and make a paste. Add 1 tbsp water if required.

2. Pat the fish pieces dry with a napkin. Make shallow cut marks on the fish pieces so that spice mix can get into the fish

3. Apply the masala paste and rub it into the fish, especially into the cut marks. Set aside for a couple of hours or at least 30 minutes to marinate.

4. Heat coconut oil in a flat pan on medium heat. Shallow fry on both sides of the fish for 2-3 minutes or until done.

5. Remove fish from the pan. Apply the lime juice on top of the fish and serve with rice.

BEEF

Like fish recipes, beef recipes also vary depending on the region the recipe originated from, the individual taste or the kinds of other spices used. The following individual spices or a combination go well with spiced fish preparations:

Spices & herbs that go with it:

- Turmeric (powder)
- Coriander (powder)
- Cinnamon
- Cardamom
- Cloves
- Fennel seeds
- Nutmeg
- Bay leaves
- Cumin (powder)
- Garlic
- Ginger
- Chili (chopped green chilies or powder)
- Black pepper
- Cayenne pepper
- Curry leaves
- Curry powder or garam masala

Most meat spice blend (meat masala) of South Asian origin include roasted ground cloves, cinnamon, cardamom, fennel, black peppercorns, nutmeg, bay leaves among others. While cooking the meat, additional spices such as coriander powder, chili powder, and cumin may be added to the above meat spice blend.

Spicy Beef and Potato Stu

Basic Ingredients

- 1-1/2 lb. beef cut into ½ inch cubes
- 3 medium potatoes, washed, peeled and cut into 1-inch cubes
- 2 tbsp – coriander powder
- 1 tbsp – cumin powder
- 1 tsp – turmeric powder
- ½ tsp – black pepper powder
- 2 green chilies slit (optional)
- 2 tsp ginger garlic paste (or 1 tsp grated ginger and 3-4 garlic crushed garlic cloves)
- 2 spring curry leaves (optional)
- 1 onion chopped
- 2 medium tomatoes chopped (optional)
- Salt to taste
-

Method

1. Sprinkle ½ teaspoon of turmeric powder, 1 tsp coriander powder, ½ tsp cumin powder and salt on

the washed and cut beef pieces, mix well and set aside for 20 minutes.

2. Instant pot set to sauté, heat oil, add onions, crushed garlic, ginger, and optional Jalapeno. Sauté till onions become translucent. Add curry leaves and mix

3. Add rest of turmeric powder, coriander powder, cumin powder, and pepper powder and mix well.

4. Add tomato and mix.

5. Now add beef pieces

6. Set one pot to meat. Cover and cook. After cooking, release the steam naturally

7. Add optional cilantro, add more salt if required depending on your taste.

Serve with rice or bread.

Recipe Note:

1. Instead of cooking in an instant pot, marinated beef may be cooked in a pressure cooker or slow cooker first and then added to sautéed onions, spices, and tomatoes and covered and allowed to simmer for 5-10 minutes.

BEEF AND CASSAVA

Ingredients

- 2 lb. beef cut into small pieces (with bone or without)

- 2 lb. cassava peeled, washed and cut into 1-inch pieces (frozen sliced cassava may be used as well)
- 2 tsp coconut oil (olive oil or vegetable oil can be used as well)
- 1/2 tsp turmeric powder
- 1-2 tsp black pepper powder
- 2 tsp coriander powder
- 2 large onion sliced
- 2-inch piece of ginger thinly sliced
- ½ - 1 tsp salt or to taste
- 2-3 medium tomato sliced
- 4-6 cloves of garlic crushed
- Cilantro – 1 cup (optional)
- ½ - 1 cup water/beef stock/bone broth

Method

1. Sprinkle ½ teaspoon of turmeric powder, 1 tsp coriander powder, ½ tsp cumin powder and salt on the washed and cut beef pieces, mix well and set aside for 20 minutes.
2. Heat oil in a pan; add onions, garlic, and ginger. Stir until golden.
3. Add coriander powder, pepper powder, and turmeric. Stir for 2-3 minutes.
4. Add tomato and mix well.
5. Add beef and cassava. Add salt. Mix well. Transfer the contents to a pressure cooker or one pot. Add sufficient water/broth (usually ¾ of a cup) so that there is enough water to build steam in the cooker.
6. Set it to meat and cook until done.

7. Release steam naturally. Garnish with cilantro and serve

Recipe Notes:

1. In most cases, water and juices from beef and cassava are enough to pressure cook the dish. But while mixing and transferring the contents to the cooker, ½ cup - 1 cup water or beef broth may be added to make sure there is enough water for pressure cooking.
2. The spices may be sautéed in an instant pot set to sauté mode or in a pressure cooker on an open stove. In that case, there is no need to transfer the contents from the sautéing pan pressure cooker.
3. Instead of a pressure cooker, a crockpot or a stovetop utensil may be used. In this case, cover the pot and cook on low-medium heat until the beef is well cooked.
4. Alternatively, cassava and beef may be cooked separately and mixed with spices. In this case, follow the steps below
    a. Cook marinated beef and set aside
    b. Cook cassava with salt (boil with sufficient water, drain) and set aside
    c. Follow steps 2,3 and 4 to make a cooked masala
    d. Add cooked beef, cassava, and mix well. Add cilantro, additional salt if needed, and serve.

BEEF PEPPER FRY

Ingredients

- 2 lb. beef cut into 1-inch cubes/strips
- 2 tsp coconut oil (olive oil or vegetable oil can be used as well)
- 1/2 tsp turmeric powder
- 1-2 tsp black pepper powder
- 2 tsp coriander powder
- 2 large onion sliced
- 2-inch piece of ginger thinly sliced
- Salt
- 2-3 medium tomato sliced
- 4-6 cloves of garlic crushed
- Cilantro – 1 cup (optional)

Method

1. Heat oil in a medium non-stick pan; add onions, garlic, and ginger. Stir until golden.
2. Add coriander powder, pepper powder, and turmeric. Stir for 2-3 minutes.
3. Add tomato and mix well.
4. Add beef and mix so that beef is coated well with spices and onion.
5. Cover and simmer for 20-25 minutes or until the beef is cooked stirring occasionally so the beef or the gravy does not stick to the pan.
6. Garnish with cilantro. Serve with rice or naan (Indian bread).

Recipe Notes:

1. The same recipe may be used to make chicken pepper fry.

CHICKEN

BELL PEPPER AND CHICKEN STIR FRY

Basic Ingredients

- 1 bell pepper washed and cut into thin slices (use the different color peppers as you desire)
- 2 tsp coconut oil (olive oil or vegetable oil can be used as well)
- 1 lb. boneless chicken breast cut into thin strips
- 1 tsp turmeric powder
- 1 tsp black pepper powder
- 1 tsp coriander powder
- 1 medium onion sliced
- ½ inch piece of ginger thinly sliced
- Salt to taste
- 1-2 medium tomato sliced
- 3 cloves of garlic crushed

Optional Ingredients

- 1 Jalapeño pepper sliced into thin pieces
- ¼ cup cilantro chopped

Method

1   Sprinkle ½ spoons of turmeric powder, pepper powder, and salt on the washed and cut chicken, mix well and set aside for 10 minutes.
2   In a pan, heat oil, add onions, crushed garlic, ginger, and optional Jalapeno. Sauté till onions become translucent.
3   Add rest of turmeric powder, coriander powder and pepper powder, and mix well.
4   Add tomato and mix.
5   Now add the bell pepper and chicken and mix well.
6   Cover and cook for 10 minutes on medium heat or until chicken and peppers are cooked. Stir occasionally.
7   Switch off the heat, add optional cilantro, add more salt if required depending on your taste.

Serve with rice or bread

COCONUT CURRY CHICKEN

Basic Ingredients

- 1-1/2 lb. chicken breast cut into small (1 inch) pieces
- 2-4 spoons of curry powder depending on your tolerance on spice
- 1 tsp turmeric
- 1` medium onion chopped
- 2-3 tsp oil
- ½ tsp pepper powder
- 2 medium potatoes – peeled and cut into 1-inch cubes
- 3-4 cloves of garlic crushed
- ½ inch cube of ginger peeled and sliced

- 1 can (14 oz) of coconut milk
- ¼ cup mint leaves or cilantro
- Salt to taste
- ½ -1 can of chicken broth (depending on the amount gravy desired)

Optional Ingredients

- 1 cup carrot sliced
- 2 medium chopped tomatoes

Method

1. Sprinkle 1 tsp curry powder, ½ tsp turmeric, and ¼ tsp salt on cut chicken. Mix well and keep it aside for 10 minutes.
2. In a separate pan, heat oil, sauté onions, garlic, and ginger until onions become translucent.
3. Add remaining curry powder, turmeric, and pepper powder. Mix for 1-2 minutes.
4. Add chicken, potato, and optional tomato and carrot. Mix well 1-2 minutes until the chicken and potato are coated with the gravy.
5. Add chicken broth and bring it to a boil. Stir well.
6. Reduce heat to low medium, cover the pan and cook for 10-12 minutes or until chicken, potato and carrots are well mixed and chicken loses its pink color and potatoes and carrots are about half cooked.
7. Add coconut milk and cover. Simmer on low heat for another 20 minutes or until chicken, potato and carrots are cooked well and soft.
8. Add mint leaves/cilantro and stir. Add salt to taste.

Switch off the heat and keep it covered for 1-2 minutes before serving.

Serve with rice or bread.

KALE AND CHICKEN FRY

This is something I tried recently and found good. The simplest way to make this is to make chicken with spices following any one of the recipes above, make kale chips and just crumble the chips into the chicken and mix well.

Ingredients

- 2 lb. boneless chicken breast/beef cut into 1-inch cubes/strips
- 2 tsp coconut oil (olive oil or vegetable oil can be used as well)
- 1/2 tsp turmeric powder
- 1-2 tsp black pepper powder
- 2 tsp coriander powder
- 2 large onion sliced
- 2-inch piece of ginger thinly sliced
- Salt to taste
- 2-3 medium tomato sliced
- 4-6 cloves of garlic crushed
- Cilantro – 1 cup (optional)
- 2 cups of green or red kale washed and cut/tore into 1-2-inch pieces (to make kale chips)

Method

1. Set instant pot to sauté setting; add coconut oil, onions, garlic, and ginger. Stir until golden.
2. Add coriander powder, pepper powder and turmeric, stir for one minute and then add tomato and mix well.
3. Add chicken mix so that chicken is coated well with spices and onion.
4. Cover the instant pot. Set to poultry and cook.
5. Meanwhile in parallel, spread the kale pieces on a cookie sheet and put in the oven at 350 degrees for 10 minutes or the kale become chips and can easily crumble.
6. Once the instant pot cooking is done. Release the pressure immediately, take the kale chips and crumble using your hand and spread it on top of chicken fry.
7. Mix well and cover it for 1 minute. Garnish with cilantro. Serve with rice or naan (Indian bread).

CHAPTER 7. SPICED RICE DISHES

TOMATO RICE

This is a good way to color your rice and also include turmeric, ginger and garlic as part of the diet. The traditional way to make this is more elaborate. However, this recipe is an easy instant pot version.

Basic Ingredients

- 2 cup basmati rice washed
- 2-1/2 cups of water
- 1 tsp turmeric powder
- 2 tsp oil
- 1 pinch black pepper powder
- 4 medium tomato chopped
- 1 medium onion chopped
- Salt to taste
- ¼ cup cilantro chopped
- 3 cloves of garlic crushed
- ½ inch piece of ginger, thinly sliced

Optional Ingredients

- ½ tsp mustard seeds
- ½ cumin seeds
- 1-2 jalapenos sliced, and seeds removed

Method

1. Cook the rice in a rice cooker or on stovetop. Drain (if needed) and set aside.
2. In a medium pan (big enough to mix rice), heat oil, and crackle optional mustard and seeds
3. Add onions, and optional garlic, ginger, and jalapenos; sauté until onion is golden brown.
4. Add turmeric and pepper and mix. Now add the tomatoes; mix,
5. Cover and cook for 10 minutes on medium heat or until tomatoes are cooked well.
6. Add the cooked rice, mix it well, and add salt to taste.
7.   Add chopped cilantro and serve.

Recipe Notes:

1. Instead of white rice, brown rice may be used. If you are using brown rice, add ½ cup more water and cook in the brown rice setting.
2. To give the rice a little more heat, use more Jalapenos or use Jalapenos with the seeds (which holds the heat).

YELLOW RICE WITH PEAS

This is another easy rice dish that can be quickly made in an instant pot. The yellow color is coming from turmeric, which is one of the healthy spices that I have extensively used in these recipes.

Basic Ingredients

- 2 cups basmati rice washed and soaked for 10 minutes
- 2-1/2 cups clear bone broth, vegetable or chicken broth
- 1 tsp turmeric powder
- 2 tsp olive or coconut oil
- 1 pinch black pepper powder
- 2 cups of frozen peas
- 1 medium onion chopped
- ¼ tsp salt
- ¼ cup cilantro chopped
- 3 cloves of garlic crushed
- ½ inch piece of ginger, thinly sliced

Optional Ingredients

- ½ tsp mustard seeds
- ½ cumin seeds
- 1-2 jalapenos sliced, and seeds removed

Method

1. Set instant pot to sauté. Add oil and crackle optional mustard and cumin seeds
2. Add onions, garlic, ginger, and optional jalapenos; sauté until onions are golden brown.
3. Add turmeric and pepper and mix. Now add the peas; mix well for a couple of minutes.
4. Now add the rice. Sauté for a minute. Add broth and salt. Mix. Close and cook on white rice setting with valve in sealing position.

5. Once the rice is cooked and steam is released naturally, open the lid, add chopped cilantro, salt to taste, and mix well. Serve hot.

Recipe Notes:

1. This recipe uses instant pot. Instead of an instant pot, a rice cooker may be used. If rice cooker is used, first thaw the peas in room temperature and cook peas along with rice in the rice cooker. Then it may be mixed with sautéed spices as in the previous recipe for tomato rice.
2. To give the rice a little more heat, use more Jalapenos or use Jalapenos with the seeds (which holds the heat).

CHAPTER 8. SPICY BROTHS AND SOUPS

SPICY VEGAN BROTH

This is a spicy version of the vegan broth that immediately helps with congestion, cold, flu, sore throat, and other ailments due to infections. Like the non-spicy version, this broth also is healing and easy for your gut. The anti-oxidants and anti-inflammatory compounds in turmeric and ginger make this broth even healthier.

Ingredients: Veggies

- 2-3 celery sticks cut into inch pieces
- 3 medium tomatoes chopped
- 1 bell green pepper cut into pieces
- 1 red bell pepper cut into pieces
- ¼ of a medium red cabbage chopped
- 1 large onion peeled and cut into 1-inch cubes
- ½ cup chopped onion (for sautéing)
- 1-pound (2-3 medium) carrots washed cut into pieces
- 1 cup kale
- 1 medium beetroot washed and cut into pieces

Ingredients – spices and herbs
- ½ cup parsley chopped
- ½ cup cilantro chopped
- 3-4 garlic cloves crushed
- 3-4 whole cloves
- 5-6 black peppercorns or ½ tsp pepper powder
- 1-2 bay leaves
- 1-inch ginger finely chopped

- 2 tsp turmeric powder or 2-inch fresh root
- 2 jalapeño pepper sliced lengthwise (seed in or out depending on your heat tolerance)
- ½ tsp cayenne powder
- ½ tsp cumin powder
- 1-gallon water
- Salt to taste (if you must or avoid salt)
- 1 tsp coconut or vegetable oil

Method

1. In a medium a pan, heat oil and add onions, crushed garlic, ginger, jalapeño peppers.

2. Sauté for 2-3 minutes or until onions become translucent. Add all the spices (cayenne, cumin, turmeric, cloves, bay leaves pepper powder) and sauté for another 2-3 minutes so the spices are blended well (make sure not to burn the spices).

3. Transfer the spice mix into a large pot (add some water to wash out any remaining spice mix from the pan and pour it into the large pot)

4. Add all the vegetables into the pot and add water, bring to a boil.

5. Lower the heat, simmer covered for about 1 hr. Stir occasionally

6. Once the vegetables are cooked, strain the broth into a large bowl

7. Add salt to taste, add some chopped fresh herbs of your choice, and serve warm.

8. Refrigerate any remaining broth

The strained-out vegetables are also nutritious and may be consumed separately.

SPICY CHICKEN BONE BROTH

This spicy bone broth immediately helps with congestion, cold, flu, sore throat, and other ailments due to infections. This broth also is healing and easy for your gut besides all the long-term health benefits that come with regular consumption of these bone broth and healing spices.

Basic Ingredients:

- 4 lb. chicken bones – any combination of wings, necks, and feet.
- 4 celery sticks cut into 1-inch pieces
- 3 medium tomatoes chopped
- 1 bell pepper cut into pieces (any color)
- 1 large onion peeled and quartered
- 1-pound (2-3 medium) carrots washed cut into pieces
- 1-gallon water
- 2 tablespoon raw unfiltered apple cider vinegar
- Salt to taste (if you must or avoid salt)

Spices & Herbs

- 2 tsp turmeric powder
- 1 tsp cumin powder or 1tsp cumin seeds
- 1 tsp coriander powder
- 1 tsp cayenne powder
- 2 tsp fenugreek seeds
- ½ cup parsley chopped

- ½ cup cilantro chopped
- ½ cup rosemary
- 3-4 garlic cloves crushed
- 3-4 whole cloves
- 2-inch ginger peeled and grated
- 5-6 black peppercorns or ½ tsp pepper powder
- 1-2 bay leaves
- 1-2 Jalapeño pepper slit (optional)

Method

1. The instant pot is set to sauté function, heat 2 tbsp olive oil, crackle cumin seeds, and fenugreek seeds. Add onions, crushed garlic, ginger, jalapeño peppers

2. Sauté for 2-3 minutes or until onions become translucent. Add all the spices (cayenne, cumin, turmeric, coriander, cloves, bay leaves, and pepper powder) and sauté for another 2-3 minutes so the spices are blended well and sufficiently roasted (make sure not to burn the spices).

3. Add all chicken bones and vegetables. Add enough water to cover all the vegetables and bones. Add vinegar.

4. Close the lid. Set the instant pot on manual setting – low pressure and 12-hour timer.

5. Once the bones and vegetables are cooked, strain the broth into a large bowl

6. Add salt to taste, add some chopped fresh herbs of your choice, and serve warm.

7. Refrigerate any remaining broth

BONE BEEF BROTH

Basic Ingredients:

- 4 lb. beef bones – a mix of marrow bones, knuckle bones, short ribs
- 4 celery stalks cut into 1-inch pieces
- 3 medium tomatoes chopped
- 1 bell pepper cut into pieces (any color)
- 1 large onion peeled and quartered
- 1-pound (2-3 medium) carrots washed cut into pieces
- 1-gallon water
- 3 tablespoon raw unfiltered apple cider vinegar
- Salt to taste (if you must or avoid salt)
- 2 tsp coconut oil

Spices & Herbs

- 2 tsp turmeric powder
- 1 tsp cumin powder or 1tsp cumin seeds
- 1 tsp coriander powder
- 1 tsp cayenne powder
- 2 tsp fenugreek seeds
- ½ cup parsley chopped
- ½ cup cilantro chopped
- ½ cup rosemary
- 3-4 garlic cloves crushed
- 3-4 whole cloves
- 2-inch ginger peeled and grated

- 5-6 black peppercorns or ½ tsp pepper powder
- 1-2 bay leaves
- 1-2 Jalapeño pepper slit (optional)

Method

1. The instant pot is set to sauté function, heat 2 tbsp olive oil, crackle cumin seeds, and fenugreek seeds. Add onions, crushed garlic, ginger, jalapeño peppers

2. Sauté for 2-3 minutes or until onions become translucent. Add all the spices (cayenne, cumin, turmeric, coriander, cloves, bay leaves and pepper powder) and sauté for another 2-3 minutes so the spices are blended well and sufficiently roasted (make sure not to burn the spices).

3. Add all chicken bones and vegetables. Add enough water to cover all the vegetables and bones. Add vinegar.

4. Close the lid. Set the instant pot on manual setting – low pressure and 12-hour timer.

5. Once the bones and vegetables are cooked, strain the broth into a large bowl

6. Add salt to taste, add some chopped fresh herbs of your choice, and serve warm.

7. Refrigerate any remaining broth

LAMB BONE BROTH (LAMB BONES ROASTED)

Ingredients

- 3 lb. lamb bones with marrow
- 1 large onion peeled quartered
- 3 medium tomatoes chopped
- 2 carrots washed cut into 1-inch long pieces
- 2 celery stalks washed and cut into 1-inch pieces
- 1-inch ginger grated
- 3-4 garlic cloves peeled and crushed
- 2-3 tbsp apple cider vinegar
- 2 tsp thyme
- ½ cup cilantro
- ¼ cup rosemary
- 1-gallon water
- salt and pepper to taste

Method

1. Set oven to 350 degrees (176 degrees Celsius) and roast the lamb bones on a cooking sheet for about 45 minutes.

2. Add all roasted bones and vegetables and other ingredients (except vinegar salt and pepper) into an instant pot and add water and vinegar

3. Set the instant pot in manual mode, select low pressure, and cooking time of 12 hrs.

4. After 12 hours, strain the broth into a large bowl. Add salt and pepper to taste. Add some fresh herbs of your choice (optional) and enjoy.

5. Refrigerate any remaining broth

BLACK BEAN SOUP

Black beans are rich in protein and is one of the healthiest of the beans/lentils family. Black beans have anti-cancer properties among other benefits.

Ingredients:

- 2 cups black beans – soaked in water overnight
- 1 bay leaf
- 3-4 garlic cloves peeled
- ½ medium red onion chopped
- 1 large tomato chopped
- ½ tsp pepper powder
- 1 tsp turmeric
- 1 tsp red pepper flakes
- 1 tsp cumin seeds
- ½ green or red bell pepper chopped
- 1 stick of celery cut
- 1 jalapeño (optional)
- 2-3 tsp taco seasoning
- 1 bunch cilantro

Method

1. The instant pot is set to sauté function, heat 2 tbsp olive oil, add cumin seeds, let it crackle. Add garlic, bay leaf, Jalapeño, ginger, onion, mix well for 1-2 minutes
2. Add turmeric, paprika, pepper powder. Sauté for another 2-3 minutes
3. Add celery, bell pepper, and celery. Mix well so the vegetables are coated with the spice mixture. Add the desired amount of water, vegetable broth, chicken broth, or bone broth.
4. Close lid and cook on beans function

5. Release the steam naturally.
6. Open the lid and add the finely chopped cilantro. Add salt to taste and enjoy warm.

LENTIL SOUP

Lentils are rich in protein and like the black bean soup from the previous recipe; the lentil soup below provides a wholesome meal especially when you are sick or recovering from sickness. These can be enjoyed as a regular meal otherwise also and is a good option when trying to eat less/lose weight and still want a nutritious meal.

Ingredients:

- 2 cups of dry lentils (any color)
- 3-4 garlic cloves peeled
- 1 medium red onion chopped
- 3 medium tomato chopped
- ½ tsp pepper powder
- 1 tsp turmeric
- ½ tsp paprika
- 1 tsp cumin seeds
- ½ green or red bell pepper
- 1 stick of celery chopped
- 1 jalapeño (optional)
- 1 tsp dried basil
- 1 bay leaf
- 1 bunch cilantro chopped
- 8 cups water/vegetable broth/chicken broth/bone broth from one of the broth recipes.
- 2 tsp olive oil

Method

1. The instant pot is set to sauté function, heat 2 tbsp olive oil, add cumin seeds, let it crackle. Add garlic, bay leaf, Jalapeño, ginger, onion, mix well for 1-2 minutes
2. Add turmeric, paprika, pepper powder. Sauté for another 2-3 minutes
3. Add celery, bell pepper, and celery. Mix well so the vegetables are coated with the spice mixture. Add the desired amount of water, vegetable broth, chicken broth, or bone broth.
4. Close lid and cook on beans function
5. Release the steam naturally.
6. Open the lid and add the finely chopped cilantro. Add salt to taste and enjoy warm.

SPICY CREAM OF BROCCOLI AND KALE SOUP

Broccoli and Kale are considered superfoods. Combine it with ginger, garlic, and turmeric – some of the best spices and some herbs and we get a healthy and nutritious soup.

Ingredients:

- 4 cups of broccoli florets
- 2 cups of kale chopped
- 3-4 garlic cloves peeled
- 1-inch ginger peeled and chopped
- 1 medium red onion chopped
- ½ tsp pepper powder
- 1 tsp turmeric
- ½ tsp paprika
- 1 tsp cumin seeds
- 1 stick of celery chopped

- 1 jalapeño (optional)
- 1 tsp dried basil
- 1 bay leaf
- 1 bunch cilantro chopped
- 8 cups water/vegetable broth/chicken broth/bone broth from one of the broth recipes.
- 2 tsp olive oil

Method
1. The instant pot is set to sauté function, heat 2 tbsp olive oil, add cumin seeds, let it crackle. Add garlic, bay leaf, Jalapeño, ginger, onion, mix well for 1-2 minutes
2. Add turmeric, paprika, and pepper powder. Sauté for another 2-3 minutes
3. Add celery, broccoli, and kale and mix well so the vegetables are coated with the spice mixture. Add the desired amount of water, vegetable broth, chicken broth or bone broth.
4. Close lid and cook on soup function
5. Release the steam naturally.
6. Transfer the soup into a blender. Add more water/broth if needed. Blend until smooth
7. Return the soup from the blender into the one pot. Heat it until it starts to boil. Mix well. Switch off the heat. Add chopped cilantro, salt to taste.

CHAPTER 9. ADDITIONAL INFORMATION

WHAT NOT TO DO WITH SPICES

While we have seen many benefits of spices and herbs, tips on usage, and cooking with it. Here are some things to be cautious about or what not to do with spices

1. **If you are planning to incorporate spices and herbs as a way of alternative treatment, consult a doctor first**

Spices and herbs with its medicinal properties could be complementary or alternative treatments to some of the health conditions based on the numerous health benefits they offer. As we now know from the study of many ancient civilizations and more recently, from indigenous people and tribes, there are many natural remedies for common ailments. In the modern world, while they may still be applied, our lifestyle is much different and we consume substances (such as medicines, alcohol, smoking etc.) which may inhibit or interact with compounds in spices and herbs. So, I recommend consulting a physician prior to any major lifestyle change using spices and herbs as an alternative to more mainstream treatments.

2. **Make sure you are not allergic to any of the spices**

Test out spices to determine if you are allergic to any of the spices. This can be done by trying out these spices in small amounts either in cooking or in drinks. You may be allergic to some spices and it can cause serious health issues. If you are using some of the spices such as cinnamon powder or turmeric for skin treatment, spot check first before using.

3. Do not burn spices while sautéing

Burned spices can not only taste bad but also cause fumes in the air that can cause coughing, watery eyes and make breathing uncomfortable. Make sure to Sautee spices in low to medium heat, use oil as a medium, and also, if required make spice paste before sautéing or sauté along with onions.

4. Some chilies can be really really pungent (hot)!

When you are dealing with chilies, it helps to understand the Scoville scale for the pungency or "heat" of the chili peppers. The Scoville scale ranges from 0 to about 4 million units. Bell peppers and pimento peppers are under 100 Scoville units while banana peppers are under 1000. Jalapeno peppers measure about 2000 – 4000 units. Always look at the label to read the Scoville level when selecting peppers.

If you eat chili that exceeds your tolerance level, it can cause an intense burning sensation in your mouth, redness, watery eyes, and cough.

5. If you are pregnant or nursing, use caution in using spices and herbs

As we have discussed earlier most spices and herbs have been in use for hundreds if not thousands of years. These have been tested over time for *normal* use to season or flavor food. While culinary use of cinnamon, turmeric, fenugreek, basil, rosemary, and thyme are considered okay, the therapeutic use of these during pregnancy is not recommended. Similarly, if you are nursing, the use of basil and cinnamon is to be avoided while garlic in culinary doses is okay but therapeutic use is not recommended.

6. Food Safety

Since spices and herbs are food, common food safety standards apply to them in packing, storing, and using them. In North America, as most of the spices are imported, one may want to make sure that the sources are reputed and the spice is pure and not altered. Also, it is recommended that the spices are cooked or sautéed first instead of using raw from the package.

7. What happens if you eat too much spice?

Eating too much spice can cause abdominal pain, burning sensation, cramps, or diarrhea. Too much spice can also result in heartburn and stomach ulcers. In some cases, too much spices and herbs can be toxic. Some spices such as nutmeg are known hallucinogenic if consumed in large quantities. If you eat too much chili or spice, below are some of the suggested remedies:

a. Drink a glass of milk or eat other dairy products like yogurt or buttermilk. Casein, the protein in milk and yogurt can break the bonds the capsaicin forms with nerve receptors helping relieve the burning sensation

b. Eat a pinch of sugar. This should help neutralize the heat from spice. Honey will help as well

c. Chocolate. Chocolate can help reduce the burning and tingling sensation caused by spice.

d. Bread. Chewing on bread can help soak up the capsaicin and keep them from sticking to nerve receptors.

WHERE TO BUY

Spice powders and blends are available in Asian stores throughout North America and Europe. All South Asian stores in major cities across the US carry these spices in powdered and whole form. Besides the brick and mortar South Asian grocery stores, there are many online stores including Amazon. For convenience a few of them are listed below:

- The Spice House https://www.thespicehouse.com
- Savory Spice https://www.savoryspiceshop.com/
- Spice Jungle https://www.spicejungle.com/
- World Spice Merchants https://www.worldspice.com
- Amazon https://www.amazon.com/Herbs-Spices-Seasonings/b?ie=UTF8&node=16310281
- American Spice Company https://www.americanspice.com/
- Spices Inc https://www.spicesinc.com/

All these stores sell individual spices by different brands and sourced from different countries as well as some spice blends.

Some of top brands are listed below:

- Savory Spice
- McCormick
- Simply Organic
- Old Bay (by McCormick)
- Goya Spices (from Goya foods)
- Lawry's Spices (by McCormick)

If you are looking for South Asian spice brands. The following are some of the top brands:

- Priya, India
- MDH, India
- Everest Spices, India
- Catch, India
- MTR Spices, India
- Eastern Spices, India
- Mother's Recipe, India
- Freelan, Sri Lanka
- Radhuni Spice, Banlgadesh
- Ramdev, India
- National, Pakistan
- Shaan, Pakistan

Besides these, there are many other local brands in these countries. You will find one or more of these brands in South Asian stores. While no two brands are the same, these brands provide an excellent selection for some of the South Asian spice blends such as curry powder, garam masala, meat masala, sambaar powder and biriyani masala among others.

Many of the Middle Eastern stores carry Mediterranean and Middle Eastern spice blends such Advieh, Baharat, Ras el

Hanout, and Harissa seasoning. The following online store I found to be a good source for these spice blends:

www.sadaf.com

www.shirazkitchen.com

www.worldspice.com

www.mypersiankitchen.com

Of course, these blends are also available on other leading online stores such as Amazon, Walmart, and many others.

REFERENCES

This book was written based on the author's personal experience with the spice as well as information from a wide range of sources. Some of the key sources are outlined below, in case the reader would like to read more details about cancer and its prevention.

Cancer

Perspectives on cancer prevention with natural compounds

http://cancerpreventionresearch.aacrjournals.org/content/6/5/387

The Amazing Cancer-Fighting Benefits of Curcumin

https://thetruthaboutcancer.com/cancer-fighting-benefits-of-curcumin/

http://www.riseearth.com/2016/06/the-amazing-cancer-fighting-benefits-of.html

Ginger is Stronger than Chemotherapy for Cancer

https://foodrevolution.org/blog/ginger-cancer-treatment/

Benefits of whole ginger extract in prostate cancer

https://www.ncbi.nlm.nih.gov/pubmed/21849094

Ginger inhibits cell growth and modulates angiogenic factors in ovarian cancer cells

https://www.ncbi.nlm.nih.gov/pubmed/18096028

Six foods that fight cancer:

http://www.foxnews.com/story/2006/04/27/six-foods-that-fight-cancer.html

The Amazing and Mighty Ginger

https://www.ncbi.nlm.nih.gov/books/NBK92775/

Phase II study of the Effects of Ginger Root Extract on Eicosanoids in Colon Mucosa in People at Normal Risk for Colorectal Cancer

https://www.ncbi.nlm.nih.gov/pmc/articles/PMC3208778/

Colon cancer: Symptoms, causes, and treatment

http://www.medicalnewstoday.com/articles/150496.php

Garlic and onions: Their cancer prevention properties

https://www.ncbi.nlm.nih.gov/pmc/articles/PMC4366009/

Garlic, onion and cereal fibre as protective factors for breast cancer: a French case-control study

https://www.ncbi.nlm.nih.gov/pubmed/9928867

Garlic and Organosulfer Compounds – Oregon State University

http://lpi.oregonstate.edu/mic/food-beverages/garlic#biological-activities-cancer-prevention

Can turmeric beat cancer – Cancer research UK

http://www.cancerresearchuk.org/about-cancer/cancers-in-general/cancer-questions/can-turmeric-prevent-bowel-cancer

Specific inhibition of cyclooxygenase-2 (COX-2) expression by dietary curcumin in HT-29 human colon cancer cells

http://www.cancerletters.info/article/S0304-3835(01)00655-3/fulltext?cc=y=

Hypertension

Garlic supplementation prevents oxidative DNA damage in essential hypertension.

https://www.ncbi.nlm.nih.gov/pubmed/16335787

Aged garlic extract lowers blood pressure in patients with treated but uncontrolled hypertension: a randomized controlled trial.

https://www.ncbi.nlm.nih.gov/pubmed/20594781

Effects of *Allium sativum* (garlic) on systolic and diastolic blood pressure in patients with essential hypertension.

https://www.ncbi.nlm.nih.gov/pubmed/24035939

Cholesterol & Blood Pressure

Lipid-lowering effects of time-released garlic powder tablets in double-blinded placebo-controlled randomized study.

https://www.ncbi.nlm.nih.gov/pubmed/19060427

Garlic for treating hypercholesterolemia. A meta-analysis of randomized clinical trials.

https://www.ncbi.nlm.nih.gov/pubmed/10975959

Investigation of the effect of ginger on the lipid levels. A double blind controlled clinical trial.

https://www.ncbi.nlm.nih.gov/pubmed/18813412

Antihyperlipidemic effects of ginger extracts in alloxan-induced diabetes and propylthiouracil-induced hypothyroidism in (rats).

https://www.ncbi.nlm.nih.gov/pubmed/23901210

Turmeric's Effects on High Blood Pressure and Cholesterol

http://www.turmeric.com/cardiovascular/turmerics-effects-on-high-blood-pressure-and-cholesterol

8 Proven Benefits of Turmeric for High Cholesterol

http://www.turmericforhealth.com/turmeric-benefits/turmeric-benefits-for-cholesterol

Cold & Flu

Preventing the common cold with a garlic supplement: a double-blind, placebo-controlled survey.

https://www.ncbi.nlm.nih.gov/pubmed/11697022

Supplementation with aged garlic extract improves both NK and γδ-T cell function and reduces the severity of cold and flu symptoms: a randomized, double-blind, placebo-controlled nutrition intervention.

https://www.ncbi.nlm.nih.gov/pubmed/22280901

Detox

Comparison of therapeutic effects of garlic and d-Penicillamine in patients with chronic occupational lead poisoning.

https://www.ncbi.nlm.nih.gov/pubmed/22151785

Pain

Comparison of effects of ginger, mefenamic acid, and ibuprofen on pain in women with primary dysmenorrhea.

https://www.ncbi.nlm.nih.gov/pubmed/19216660

Daily Ginger Consumption Found to Ease Muscle Pain

http://www.medicalnewstoday.com/articles/189359.php

Arthritis

http://www.arthritis.org/living-with-arthritis/treatments/natural/supplements-herbs/guide/turmeric.php

Infections

https://www.ncbi.nlm.nih.gov/pubmed/18814211

https://www.ncbi.nlm.nih.gov/pubmed/18814211

https://www.ncbi.nlm.nih.gov/pubmed/23123794

Diabetes & Blood Sugar

https://www.ncbi.nlm.nih.gov/pmc/articles/PMC4277626/

Neuroprotective Properties

http://www.eurekaselect.com/76132

http://www.nature.com/articles/srep38846

http://articles.mercola.com/sites/articles/archive/2013/07/08/-vs-drugs-for-parkinsons.aspx

http://www.sciencedirect.com/science/article/pii/S1357272508002550

Turmeric & Circulation

https://www.multivitaminguide.org/blog/-benefits-unclogs-arteries-improves-blood-circulation/

Anti-Inflammatory

https://www.ncbi.nlm.nih.gov/pubmed/19594223

https://www.ncbi.nlm.nih.gov/pubmed/12676044

DISCLAIMER

This book details the author's personal experiences in using Indian spices and the information contained in the public domain as well as the the author's opinion. The author is not licensed as a doctor, nutritionist or chef. The author is providing this book and its contents on an "as is" basis and makes no representations or warranties of any kind with respect to this book or its contents. The author disclaims all such representations and warranties, including for example warranties of merchantability and educational or medical advice for a particular purpose. In addition, the author does not represent or warrant that the information accessible via this book is accurate, complete or current. The statements made about products and services have not been evaluated by the US FDA or any equivalent organization in other countries.

The author will not be liable for damages arising out of or in connection with the use of this book or the information contained within. This is a comprehensive limitation of liability that applies to all damages of any kind, including (without limitation) compensatory; direct, indirect or consequential damages; loss of data, income or profit; loss of or damage to property and claims of third parties. It is understood that this book is not intended as a substitute for consultation with a licensed medical or a culinary professional. Before starting any lifestyle changes, it is recommended that you consult a licensed professional to ensure that you are doing what's best for your situation.

The use of this book implies your acceptance of this disclaimer.

Thank You

If you enjoyed this book or found it useful, I would greatly appreciate if you could post a short review on Amazon. I read all the reviews and your feedback will help me to make this book even better. For your convenience, please click the following link to take you directly to Amazon where you can post the review.

PREVIEW OF OTHER BOOKS IN THIS SERIES

ESSENTIAL SPICES AND HERBS: TURMERIC

Turmeric is truly a wonder spice. It has anti-inflammatory, anti-oxidant, anti-cancer, and anti-bacterial properties. Find out the amazing benefits of turmeric. Includes many recipes for incorporating turmeric in your daily life.

Turmeric is a spice known to man for thousands of years and has been used for cooking, food preservation, and as a natural remedy for common ailments. This book explains:

- Many health benefits of turmeric including fighting cancer, inflammation, and pain.
- Turmeric as beauty treatments - turmeric masks
- Recipes for teas, smoothies and dishes
- References and links to a number of research studies on the effectiveness of turmeric

Essential Spices and Herbs: Turmeric is a quick read and offers a lot of concise information. A great tool to have in your alternative therapies and healthy lifestyle toolbox!

PREVENTING CANCER

 World Health Organization (WHO) estimates more than half of all cancer incidents are preventable.

Cancer is one of the most fearsome diseases to strike mankind. There has been much research into both conventional and alternative therapies for different kinds of cancers. Different cancers require different treatment options and offer a different prognosis. While there has been significant progress in recent times in cancer research towards a cure, there are none available currently. However, more than half of all cancers are likely preventable through modifications in lifestyle and diet.

Preventing Cancer offers a quick insight into cancer-causing factors, foods that fight cancer, and how the three spices, turmeric, ginger and garlic, can not only spice up your food but potentially make all your food into cancer fighting meals. While there are many other herbs and spices that help fight cancer, these three spices work together and complementarily. In addition, the medicinal value of these spices has been proven over thousands of years of use. The book includes:

- Cancer-causing factors and how to avoid them
- Top 12 cancer-fighting foods, the cancers they fight and how to incorporate them into your diet

- Cancer-fighting properties of turmeric, ginger and garlic
- Over 30 recipes including teas, smoothies and other dishes that incorporate these spices
- References and links to many research studies on the effectiveness of these spices.

PREVENTING ALZHEIMER'S

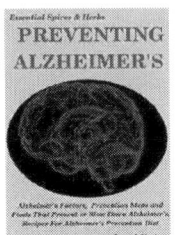Approximately 50 million people suffer from Alzheimer's worldwide. In the U.S. alone, 5.5 million people have Alzheimer's – about 10 percent of the worldwide Alzheimer's population.

Alzheimer's disease is a progressive brain disorder that damages and eventually destroys brain cells, leading to memory loss, changes in thinking, and other brain functions. While the rate of progressive decline in brain function is slow at the onset, it gets worse with time and age. Brain function decline accelerates, and brain cells eventually die over time. While there has been significant research done to find a cure, currently there is no cure available.

Alzheimer's incidence rate in the U.S. and other western countries is significantly higher than that of the countries in the developing world. Factors such as lifestyle, diet, physical and mental activity, and social engagement play a part in the development and progression of Alzheimer's

In most cases, if you are above the age of 50, plaques and tangles associated with Alzheimer's may have already started forming in your brain. At the age of 65, you have a 10% chance of Alzheimer's and at age 80, the chances are about 50%.

With lifestyle changes, proper diet and exercise (of the mind and body), Alzheimer's is preventable.

In recent times, Alzheimer's is beginning to reach epidemic proportions. The cost of Alzheimer's to the US economy is expected to cross a trillion dollars in 10 years. It is a serious health care issue in many of the western countries as the population age and the life expectancy increase.

At this time, our understanding of what causes Alzheimer's and the ways to treat it is at its infancy. However, we know the factors that affect Alzheimer's and we can use that knowledge to prevent, delay the onset or at least slow down the rate of progression of the disease.

While this book does not present all the answers, it is an attempt to examines the factors affecting Alzheimer's and how to reduce the risk of developing Alzheimer's. A combination of diet and both mental and physical exercise is believed to help in prevention or reducing risk. The book includes:

Discussion on factors in Alzheimer's development

The list of foods that help protect the brain and boost brain health is included in the book:

Over 30 recipes including teas, smoothies, broths, and other dishes that incorporate brain-boosting foods:

References and links to several research studies on Alzheimer's and brain foods.

ALL NATURAL WELLNESS DRINKS

 It contains 35 recipes for wellness drinks that include teas, smoothies, soups, and vegan & bone broths. The recipes in this book are unique and combine superfoods, medicinal spices, and herbs. These drinks are anti-cancer, anti-diabetic, ant-aging, heart healthy, anti-inflammatory, and anti-oxidant as well as promote weight loss.

By infusing nature-based nutrients (super fruits and vegetables, spices, and herbs) into drink recipes, we get some amazing wellness drinks that not only replace water loss but nourish the body with vitamins, essential metals, anti-oxidants, and many other nutrients. These drinks may be further enhanced by incorporating spices and herbs along with other superfoods. These drinks not only help heal the body but also enhance the immune system to help prevent many forms of diseases. These drinks may also help rejuvenate the body and delay the aging process. The book also includes suggested wellness drinks for common ailments.

INTRODUCTION TO CURRY

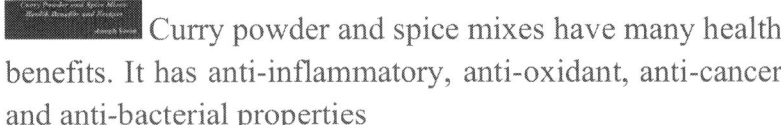 Curry powder and spice mixes have many health benefits. It has anti-inflammatory, anti-oxidant, anti-cancer and anti-bacterial properties

120

Curry is becoming a popular dish worldwide. Not only curry is delicious, but it also provides immense health benefits.

Curry powder contains turmeric, chili powder, coriander, and cumin among others. They are all known to have immense health benefits. This book includes:

- History of curry and curry powder
- Health benefits of each ingredient
- How to make various curry powder and curry paste mixes including Indian, Thai, and Ethiopian curry mixes
- Several recipes for making Indian and Thai curries

ESSENTIAL SPICES AND HERBS: GINGER

Ginger is a spice known to man for thousands of years and has been used for cooking and as a natural remedy for common ailments. Recent studies have shown that ginger has anti-cancer, anti-inflammatory, and anti-oxidant properties. Ginger helps in reducing muscle pain and is an excellent remedy for nausea. Ginger promotes a healthy digestive system. The book details:

- Many health benefits of ginger including fighting cancer, inflammation, pain and nausea
- Remedies using ginger
- Recipes for teas, smoothies, and other dishes
- References and links to a number of research studies on the effectiveness of ginger

ESSENTIAL SPICES AND HERBS: GARLIC

 Garlic is one of the worlds healthiest foods. It helps in maintaining a healthy heart, an excellent remedy for common inflections and has both anti-oxidant and anti-inflammatory properties. It is an excellent food supplement that provides some key vitamins and minerals. This book details the benefits of garlic and describes many easy recipes for incorporating garlic into the diet:

- Many health benefits of garlic including fighting cancer, inflammation, heart health and more
- Remedies using garlic
- Recipes for teas, smoothies, and other dishes
- References and links to a number of research studies on the effectiveness of garlic

ESSENTIAL SPICES AND HERBS: CINNAMON

Cinnamon is an essential spice. It has Anti-diabetic, anti-inflammatory, anti-oxidant, anti-cancer and anti-infections and neuroprotective properties. Cinnamon is a spice known to man for thousands of years and has been used for food preservation, baking, cooking, and as a natural remedy for common ailments. Recent studies have shown that cinnamon has important medicinal properties. This book explains:

- Many health benefits of cinnamon including anti-diabetic, neuroprotective and others.
- Recipes for teas, smoothies, and other dishes
- References and links to a number of research studies on the effectiveness of cinnamon

ANTI-CANCER CURRIES

It is estimated that more than 50% of the cancer incidents are preventable by changing lifestyles, controlling or avoiding cancer-causing factors, or simply eating healthy. There are several foods that are known to have anti-cancer properties either directly or indirectly. Some of these have properties that inhibit cancer cell growth while others have anti-oxidant and anti-inflammatory properties that contribute to overall health. However, many spices and herbs have direct anti-cancer properties and when one uses anti-cancer spices and herbs in cooking fresh food, there is an immense benefit to be gained. Curry dishes are cooked using many spices that have anti-oxidant, anti-inflammatory, and anti-cancer properties.

This book contains 30 curry recipes that use healthy and anti-cancer ingredients. These recipes are simple and take an average of 20-30 minutes to prepare.

BEGINNERS GUIDE TO COOKING WITH SPICES

Have you ever wondered how to cook with spices? Learn about the many benefits of spices and how to cook with them!

Find out how to start using spices as seasoning and healthy foods. Includes sample recipes,

Beginner's guide to cooking with spices is an introductory book that explains the history, various uses, and their medicinal properties and health benefits. The book details how they may be easily incorporated in everyday cooking. The book will cover the following:

- Health benefits of spices and herbs
- Spice mixes from around the world and their uses
- Tips for cooking with Spices
- Cooking Vegan with Spices
- Cooking Meat and Fish with spices
- Spiced Rice Dishes
- Spicy Soups and Broths

EASY INDIAN INSTANT POT COOKBOOK

Instant Pot or Electric Pressure Cooker is the most important cooking device in my kitchen. It saves me time, energy, and helps me prepare hassle-free Indian meals all the time.

The Easy Indian Instant Pot Meals contains includes:

- Recipes for 50 Indian dishes
- Tips for cooking with Instant Pot or any electric pressure cooker
- General tips for cooking with spices

FIGHTING THE VIRUS: HOW TO BOOST YOUR BODY'S IMMUNE RESPONSE AND FIGHT VIRUS NATURALLY

What can we do to improve our health and immune response so that our bodies are less prone to viral or bacterial infections? How can we enable our body for a speedy recovery in case of getting such infections?

The answer lies in lifestyle changes that include better hygiene practices, exercise, sleep, and a better diet to keep our body in optimum health. This book is focused on understanding the body's immune system, factors that improve the body's immune response and some natural remedies and recipes. The book contains:

•Overview of the human immune system
•Factors affecting immune response
•Natural substances that fight viral, fungal and bacterial infections
•Recipes that may improve immunity and help speedy recovery
•Supplements that may help improve the immune system
•Scientific studies and references

Easy Spicy Eggs: All Natural Easy and Spicy Egg Recipes

Recipes in this book are not a collection of authentic dishes, but a spicy version of chicken recipes that are easy to make and 100% healthy and flavorful. Ingredients used are mostly natural without any preserved or processed foods.

Most of these recipes include tips and tricks to vary and adapt to your taste of spice level or make with some of the ingredients you like other than the prescribed ingredients in the recipes.

There are about 30 recipes in the book with ideas to make another 30 or even more with the suggestions and notes included with many of the recipes. Cooking does not have to be prescriptive but can be creative. I invite you to try your own variations and apply your creativity to cook dishes that are truly your own.

Food for the Brain

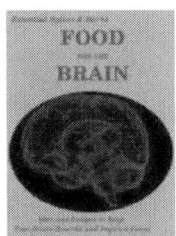Nature provides for foods that nourish both the body and the brain. Most often the focus of the diet is physical nourishment, - muscle building, weight loss, energy, athletic

performance, and many others. Similar to foods that help the body, there are many foods that help the brain, improve memory and help slow down the aging process. While it is normal to have your physical and mental abilities somewhat slow down with age, diseases such as Alzheimer's, and Parkinson's impact these declines even more. Brain function decline accelerates, and more and more brain cells eventually die over time.

With regular exercises, strength training, practicing martial arts and other physical activities can arrest the physical decline. This book's primary focus is on managing decline in mental and brain function through diet and contains the following:
Characteristics of foods that helps in keeping your brain healthy and young. Brain healthy foods including meats, fruits, vegetables, spices, herbs, and seafood. Supplements to improve memory, cognition and support brain health
Mediterranean diet recipe ideas
DASH diet recipe ideas
Asian diet recipe ideas
Brain boosting supplements and recommendations products and dosage
References

Printed in Great Britain
by Amazon